the
clayton m.
christensen
reader

SELECTED ARTICLES FROM THE
WORLD'S FOREMOST AUTHORITY
ON **DISRUPTIVE INNOVATION**

the clayton m. christensen reader

Harvard Business Review Press

Boston, Massachusetts

Christensen, Clayton M., author.
   The Clayton M. Christensen reader.
Boston, Massachusetts: Harvard Business Review Press, [2015]
LCCN 2015037447
   ISBN 9781633690998 (alk. paper)
LCSH: Management. Creative ability in business. Technological innovations. Organizational change.
LCC HD31 .C5224 2015 DDC 658—dc23 LC record available at http://lccn.loc.gov/2015037447

ISBN: 9781633690998
eISBN: 9781633691001

Contents

the
clayton m.
christensen
reader

Clayton M. Christensen is best known for his theory of disruptive innovation, in which he warns large, established companies of the danger of becoming *too* good at what they do best. To grow profit margins and revenue, he observes, such companies tend to develop products to satisfy the demands of their most sophisticated customers. As successful as this strategy may be, it means that those companies also tend to ignore opportunities to meet the needs of less sophisticated customers—who may eventually form much larger markets. An upstart can therefore introduce a simpler product that is cheaper and thus becomes more widely adopted (a "disruptive innovation"). Through incremental innovation, that product is refined and moves upmarket, completing the disruption of the original company.

Christensen's work on disruption is nuanced and often misunderstood. Not every hugely innovative technology is "disruptive" (though you wouldn't know that from the way journalists and tech enthusiasts throw the word around). Not every start-up will beat the incumbent. Not every big company is going to be disrupted. Reading Christensen's original *Harvard Business Review* articles on disruption yields a more accurate picture of his theory and how businesses can prepare for and overcome the threat he describes.

Much of that picture comes from the case studies embedded in each article. Christensen is a deliberate storyteller, and his business examples serve as parables; compelling and memorable, they give readers the context to apply his ideas to their own industries. Those who know Christensen's work are familiar with the success of steel minimills (disrupters!) and the fate of Digital Equipment Corporation (disrupted!); they know what goes into the creation of the best milk shake (a product with a job to do) and why the iPod was the MP3 player that really took off (an innovative business model). In "How Will You Measure Your Life?" Christensen reflects on his use of storytelling to persuade one powerful CEO to change strategy and go to the bottom of the market. "If I'd been suckered into telling Andy Grove what he should think about the microprocessor business, I'd have been killed. But instead of telling him what to think, I [told him the story of the minimills and] taught him how to think." Christensen's articles do the same for readers.

This volume collects the most essential and influential of Christensen's HBR articles. In them, Christensen examines many different pieces of the disruption puzzle. Understanding those pieces is critical for strategy teams, product development units, and organizational leaders. They include:

The threat of disruptive innovation: the core theory of why bad things happen to good companies. **"Disruptive Technologies: Catching the Wave"** is the big-picture "why this is a problem" article warning established companies that a seemingly rational concern with profit margins can have disastrous results. It outlines several classic examples—primarily disk drives, along with Apple and Digital Equipment Corporation—to show that there is a pattern big companies should pay attention to.

Organizational structure: **"Meeting the Challenge of Disruptive Change"** describes how leaders can structure their organizations to allow the kinds of innovation that stave off disruption. Here Christensen runs Digital Equipment Corporation through his framework to show how it can be used to explain that company's infamous reverse of fortune.

Product innovation: **"Marketing Malpractice: The Cause and the Cure"** again asks why good managers struggle to innovate successfully, this time focusing on the discipline of product innovation itself rather than on organizational and management structures. By understanding the tasks that customers look to a product for (the "job to be done"), a company can develop offerings—products, services, and whole brands—that customers truly value. Christensen uses the "milk shake" example to show how product developers should be considering their task.

The financial tools in the way: Established financial incentives often make it unattractive for companies to innovate. In **"Innovation Killers: How Financial Tools Destroy Your Capacity to Do New Things,"** Christensen and his coauthors target metrics such as discounted cash flow, net present value, and earnings per share, along with attitudes toward fixed and sunk costs. They suggest that leaders take up other methods for evaluating investments—ones that consider future value.

Business model innovation: Product innovations might be necessary, but to be truly disruptive, they often need to be delivered to the market through new business models. In **"Reinventing Your Business Model,"** Christensen and his coauthors describe how to determine if your company needs a new business model and what makes one successful, using examples ranging from Apple's iTunes to CVS's MinuteClinics.

The role of business models in M&A: To reinvent their business models, companies sometimes decide to merge with or acquire another firm. But the failure rate of M&A is somewhere between 70% and 90%. **"The New M&A Playbook"** explains that the failures often stem from a lack of clarity about why a merger or an acquisition is being pursued. Companies need to consider whether they are really after business model reinvention or are simply looking to bolster their current model. These purposes demand very different implementations of a deal—from paying the right price to determining how employees and other resources will be handled.

Where your industry's future growth lies: If disruption is predictable, we should be able to step back and look at markets as a whole to understand how disruption will change an industry over time. **"Skate to Where the Money Will Be"** describes a pattern of evolution of markets and industries that can help managers see where their next source of profits will be—so that they don't find themselves outpaced by another company in that new sphere.

The extendable core: How do you know how big a particular threat to your business actually is? **"Surviving Disruption"** helps you calculate the strengths of your potential disrupter's business model along with your own relative advantages and determine what conditions could keep your disrupter from triumphing. Christensen and his coauthor build on the jobs-to-be-done theory and introduce the "extendable core"—the part of a disrupter's business model that enables it to keep undercutting you as it creeps upmarket into your territory.

Disruptive innovation, revisited: The ideas summed up in the phrase "disruptive innovation" have become a powerful part of business thinking in the 20 years since they were introduced—but they're in danger of losing their usefulness, because they've been misunderstood and misapplied. In **"What Is Disruptive Innovation?"** Christensen and his coauthors revisit the essential concepts, show the importance of using the term precisely, and share what they have learned from two decades' application of the idea in the field.

What makes good management theory: By testing a business theory with the scientific method—by conducting a reality check—we can learn whether the theory will really help us predict the future. **"Why Hard-Nosed Executives Should Care About Management Theory"** argues for more-rigorous testing of theories so that managers can gain a better sense of whether an idea is relevant to their specific situation.

A personal strategy: Christensen extends his examination to the personal realm, arguing that bad things sometimes happen to good people because those people lack a strategy for their lives. In **"How Will You Measure Your Life?"** he uses concepts from business to challenge readers to manage their careers and personal lives in a way that leads to lasting satisfaction.

To Christensen, the role of every general manager is to lay a foundation for future growth. To that end, managers need to understand disruptive innovation, the threat it poses, and how to lead their teams and organizations to create growth that can keep pace with ever-evolving technologies, industries, and customers.

—The Editors

Disruptive Technologies

Catching the Wave. *by Joseph L. Bower and Clayton M. Christensen*

ONE OF THE MOST CONSISTENT patterns in business is the failure of leading companies to stay at the top of their industries when technologies or markets change. Goodyear and Firestone entered the radial-tire market quite late. Xerox let Canon create the small-copier market. Bucyrus-Erie allowed Caterpillar and Deere to take over the mechanical excavator market. Sears gave way to Wal-Mart.

The pattern of failure has been especially striking in the computer industry. IBM dominated the mainframe market but missed by years the emergence of minicomputers, which were technologically much simpler than mainframes. Digital Equipment dominated the minicomputer market with innovations like its VAX architecture but missed the personal-computer market almost completely. Apple Computer led the world of personal computing and established the standard for user-friendly computing but lagged five years behind the leaders in bringing its portable computer to market.

Why is it that companies like these invest aggressively—and successfully—in the technologies necessary to retain their current customers but then fail to make certain other technological investments that customers of the future will demand? Undoubtedly, bureaucracy, arrogance, tired executive blood, poor planning, and short-term investment horizons have all played a role. But a more fundamental reason lies at the heart of the paradox: leading companies succumb to one of the most popular, and valuable, management dogmas. They stay close to their customers.

Although most managers like to think they are in control, customers wield extraordinary power in directing a company's investments. Before managers decide to launch a technology, develop a product, build a plant, or establish new channels of distribution, they must look to their customers first: Do their customers want it? How big will the market be? Will the investment be profitable? The more astutely managers ask and answer these questions, the more completely their investments will be aligned with the needs of their customers.

This is the way a well-managed company should operate. Right? But what happens when customers reject a new technology, product concept, or way of doing business because it does *not* address their needs as effectively as a company's current approach? The large photocopying centers that represented the core of Xerox's customer base at first had no use for small, slow tabletop copiers. The excavation contractors that had relied on Bucyrus-Erie's big-bucket steam- and diesel-powered cable shovels didn't want hydraulic excavators because initially they were small and weak. IBM's large commercial, government, and industrial customers saw no immediate use for minicomputers. In each instance, companies listened to their customers, gave them the product performance they were looking for, and, in the end, were hurt by the very technologies their customers led them to ignore.

We have seen this pattern repeatedly in an ongoing study of leading companies in a variety of industries that have confronted technological change. The research shows that most well-managed, established companies are consistently ahead of their industries in developing and commercializing new technologies—from incremental improvements to radically new approaches—as long as those technologies address the next-generation performance needs of their customers. However, these same companies are rarely in the forefront of commercializing new technologies that don't initially meet the needs of mainstream customers and appeal only to small or emerging markets.

Idea in Brief

Goodyear, Xerox, Bucyrus-Erie, Digital. Leading companies all—yet they all failed to stay at the top of their industries when technologies or markets changed radically. That's disturbing enough, but the reason for the failure is downright alarming. The very processes that successful, well-managed companies use to serve the rapidly growing needs of their current customers can leave them highly vulnerable when market-changing technologies appear.

When a technology that has the potential for revolutionizing an industry emerges, established companies typically see it as unattractive: it's not something their mainstream customers want, and its projected profit margins aren't sufficient to cover big-company cost structures. As a result, the new technology tends to get ignored in favor of what's currently popular with the best customers. But then another company steps in to bring the innovation to a new market. Once the disruptive technology becomes established there, smaller-scale innovations rapidly raise the technology's performance on attributes that *mainstream* customers value.

What happens next is akin to the rapid, final moves leading to checkmate. The new technology invades the established market. By the time the established supplier—with its high overhead and profit margin requirements—wakes up and smells the coffee, its competitive disadvantage is insurmountable.

Using the rational, analytical investment processes that most well-managed companies have developed, it is nearly impossible to build a cogent case for diverting resources from known customer needs in established markets to markets and customers that seem insignificant or do not yet exist. After all, meeting the needs of established customers and fending off competitors takes all the resources a company has, and then some. In well-managed companies, the processes used to identify customers' needs, forecast technological trends, assess profitability, allocate resources across competing proposals for investment, and take new products to market are focused—for all the right reasons—on current customers and markets. These processes are designed to weed out proposed products and technologies that do *not* address customers' needs.

In fact, the processes and incentives that companies use to keep focused on their main customers work so well that they blind those companies to important new technologies in emerging markets.

Idea in Practice

At issue here is a key distinction:

- **Sustaining innovation** maintains a steady rate of product improvement.

- **Disruptive innovation** often sacrifices performance along dimensions that are important to current customers and offers a very different package of attributes that are not (yet) valued by those customers. At the same time, the new attributes can open up entirely new markets. For example, Sony's early transistor radios sacrificed sound fidelity, but they created a new market for small, portable radios.

Staying focused on your main customers can work so well that you overlook disruptive technologies. The consequences can be far more disastrous than a missed opportunity. Case in point: not one of the independent hard-disk drive companies that existed in 1976 is still around today.

To prevent disruptive technologies from slipping through their fingers, established organizations must learn how to identify and nurture innovations on a more modest scale—so that small orders are meaningful, ill-defined markets have time to mature, and

Many companies have learned the hard way the perils of ignoring new technologies that do not initially meet the needs of mainstream customers. For example, although personal computers did not meet the requirements of mainstream minicomputer users in the early 1980s, the computing power of the desktop machines improved at a much faster rate than minicomputer users' *demands* for computing power did. As a result, personal computers caught up with the computing needs of many of the customers of Wang, Prime, Nixdorf, Data General, and Digital Equipment. Today they are performance-competitive with minicomputers in many applications. For the minicomputer makers, keeping close to mainstream customers and ignoring what were initially low-performance desktop technologies used by seemingly insignificant customers in emerging markets was a rational decision—but one that proved disastrous.

The technological changes that damage established companies are usually not radically new or difficult from a *technological* point of view. They do, however, have two important characteristics: First, they typically present a different package of performance attributes—ones that, at least at the outset, are not valued by existing overhead is low enough to permit early profits. Here's a four-step guide:

1. **Determine whether the technology is disruptive or sustaining.** Ask the technical folks—they're more attuned than marketing and financial managers to which technologies have the potential to revolutionize the market.

2. **Define the strategic significance of the disruptive technology.** Your best customers are the last people to ask about this—sustaining technologies are what they care about.

3. **Locate the initial market for the disruptive technology.** If the market doesn't yet exist, conventional market research won't give you the information you need. So create it instead, by experimenting rapidly, iteratively, and inexpensively— with both the product and the market.

4. **House the disruptive technology in an independent entity.** For a disruptive technology to thrive, it can't be required to compete with established products for company resources.

customers. Second, the performance attributes that existing customers do value improve at such a rapid rate that the new technology can later invade those established markets. Only at this point will mainstream customers want the technology. Unfortunately for the established suppliers, by then it is often too late: the pioneers of the new technology dominate the market.

It follows, then, that senior executives must first be able to spot the technologies that seem to fall into this category. Next, to commercialize and develop the new technologies, managers must protect them from the processes and incentives that are geared to serving established customers. And the only way to protect them is to create organizations that are completely independent from the mainstream business.

No industry demonstrates the danger of staying too close to customers more dramatically than the hard-disk-drive industry. Between 1976 and 1992, disk-drive performance improved at a stunning rate: the physical size of a 100-megabyte (MB) system shrank from 5,400 to 8 cubic inches, and the cost per MB fell from $560 to $5. Technological change, of course, drove these breathtaking achievements.

About half of the improvement came from a host of radical advances that were critical to continued improvements in disk-drive performance; the other half came from incremental advances.

The pattern in the disk-drive industry has been repeated in many other industries: the leading, established companies have consistently led the industry in developing and adopting new technologies that their customers demanded—even when those technologies required completely different technological competencies and manufacturing capabilities from the ones the companies had. In spite of this aggressive technological posture, no single disk-drive manufacturer has been able to dominate the industry for more than a few years. A series of companies have entered the business and risen to prominence, only to be toppled by newcomers who pursued technologies that at first did not meet the needs of mainstream customers. As a result, not one of the independent disk-drive companies that existed in 1976 survives today.

To explain the differences in the impact of certain kinds of technological innovations on a given industry, the concept of *performance trajectories*—the rate at which the performance of a product has improved, and is expected to improve, over time—can be helpful. Almost every industry has a critical performance trajectory. In mechanical excavators, the critical trajectory is the annual improvement in cubic yards of earth moved per minute. In photocopiers, an important performance trajectory is improvement in number of copies per minute. In disk drives, one crucial measure of performance is storage capacity, which has advanced 50% each year on average for a given size of drive.

Different types of technological innovations affect performance trajectories in different ways. On the one hand, *sustaining* technologies tend to maintain a rate of improvement; that is, they give customers something more or better in the attributes they already value. For example, thin-film components in disk drives, which replaced conventional ferrite heads and oxide disks between 1982 and 1990, enabled information to be recorded more densely on disks. Engineers had been pushing the limits of the performance they could wring from ferrite heads and oxide disks, but the drives employing these technologies seemed to have reached the natural limits of an *S* curve. At that point, new thin-film technologies emerged that restored—or sustained—the historical trajectory of performance improvement.

On the other hand, *disruptive* technologies introduce a very different package of attributes from the one mainstream customers historically value, and they often perform far worse along one or two dimensions that are particularly important to those customers. As a rule, mainstream customers are unwilling to use a disruptive product in applications they know and understand. At first, then, disruptive technologies tend to be used and valued only in new markets or new applications; in fact, they generally make possible the emergence of new markets. For example, Sony's early transistor radios sacrificed sound fidelity but created a market for portable radios by offering a new and different package of attributes—small size, light weight, and portability.

In the history of the hard-disk-drive industry, the leaders stumbled at each point of disruptive technological change: when the diameter of disk drives shrank from the original 14 inches to 8 inches, then to 5.25 inches, and finally to 3.5 inches. Each of these new architectures initially offered the market substantially less storage capacity than the typical user in the established market required. For example, the 8-inch drive offered 20 MB when it was introduced, while the primary market for disk drives at that time—mainframes—required 200 MB on average. Not surprisingly, the leading computer manufacturers rejected the 8-inch architecture at first. As a result, their suppliers, whose mainstream products consisted of 14-inch drives with more than 200 MB of capacity, did not pursue the disruptive products aggressively. The pattern was repeated when the 5.25-inch and 3.5-inch drives emerged: established computer makers rejected the drives as inadequate, and, in turn, their disk-drive suppliers ignored them as well.

But while they offered less storage capacity, the disruptive architectures created other important attributes—internal power supplies and smaller size (8-inch drives); still smaller size and low-cost stepper motors (5.25-inch drives); and ruggedness, light weight, and low-power consumption (3.5-inch drives). From the late 1970s to the mid-1980s, the availability of the three drives made possible the development of new markets for minicomputers, desktop PCs, and portable computers, respectively.

Although the smaller drives represented disruptive technological change, each was technologically straightforward. In fact, there were engineers at many leading companies who championed the new technologies and built working prototypes with bootlegged resources before management gave a formal go-ahead. Still, the leading companies could not move the products through their organizations and into the market in a timely way. Each time a disruptive technology emerged, between one-half and two-thirds of the established manufacturers failed to introduce models employing the new architecture—in stark contrast to their timely launches of critical sustaining technologies. Those companies that finally did launch new models typically lagged behind entrant companies by two years—eons in an industry whose products' life cycles are often two years. Three waves of entrant companies led these revolutions; they first captured the new markets and then dethroned the leading companies in the mainstream markets.

How could technologies that were initially inferior and useful only to new markets eventually threaten leading companies in established markets? Once the disruptive architectures became established in their new markets, sustaining innovations raised each architecture's performance along steep trajectories—so steep that the performance available from each architecture soon satisfied the needs of customers in the established markets. For example, the 5.25-inch drive, whose initial 5 MB of capacity in 1980 was only a fraction of the capacity that the minicomputer market needed, became fully performance-competitive in the minicomputer market by 1986 and in the mainframe market by 1991. (See the graph "How disk-drive performance met market needs.")

A company's revenue and cost structures play a critical role in the way it evaluates proposed technological innovations. Generally, disruptive technologies look financially unattractive to established

How disk-drive performance met market needs

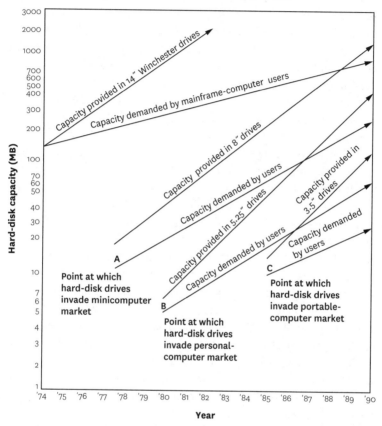

companies. The potential revenues from the discernible markets are small, and it is often difficult to project how big the markets for the technology will be over the long term. As a result, managers typically conclude that the technology cannot make a meaningful contribution to corporate growth and, therefore, that it is not worth the management effort required to develop it. In addition, established companies have often installed higher cost structures to serve sustaining technologies than those required by disruptive technologies.

As a result, managers typically see themselves as having two choices when deciding whether to pursue disruptive technologies. One is to go *downmarket* and accept the lower profit margins of the emerging markets that the disruptive technologies will initially serve. The other is to go *upmarket* with sustaining technologies and enter market segments whose profit margins are alluringly high. (For example, the margins of IBM's mainframes are still higher than those of PCs). Any rational resource-allocation process in companies serving established markets will choose going upmarket rather than going down.

Managers of companies that have championed disruptive technologies in emerging markets look at the world quite differently. Without the high cost structures of their established counterparts, these companies find the emerging markets appealing. Once the companies have secured a foothold in the markets and improved the performance of their technologies, the established markets above them, served by high-cost suppliers, look appetizing. When they do attack, the entrant companies find the established players to be easy and unprepared opponents because the opponents have been looking upmarket themselves, discounting the threat from below.

It is tempting to stop at this point and conclude that a valuable lesson has been learned: managers can avoid missing the next wave by paying careful attention to potentially disruptive technologies that do *not* meet current customers' needs. But recognizing the pattern and figuring out how to break it are two different things. Although entrants invaded established markets with new technologies three times in succession, none of the established leaders in the disk-drive industry seemed to learn from the experiences of those that fell before them. Management myopia or lack of foresight cannot explain these failures. The problem is that managers keep doing what has worked in the past: serving the rapidly growing needs of their current customers. The processes that successful, well-managed companies have developed to allocate resources among proposed investments are *incapable* of funneling resources into programs that current customers explicitly don't want and whose profit margins seem unattractive.

Managing the development of new technology is tightly linked to a company's investment processes. Most strategic proposals—to add capacity or to develop new products or processes—take shape at the lower levels of organizations in engineering groups or project teams. Companies then use analytical planning and budgeting systems to select from among the candidates competing for funds. Proposals to create new businesses in emerging markets are particularly challenging to assess because they depend on notoriously unreliable estimates of market size. Because managers are evaluated on their ability to place the right bets, it is not surprising that in well-managed companies, mid- and top-level managers back projects in which the market seems assured. By staying close to lead customers, as they have been trained to do, managers focus resources on fulfilling the requirements of those reliable customers that can be served profitably. Risk is reduced—and careers are safeguarded—by giving known customers what they want.

Seagate Technology's experience illustrates the consequences of relying on such resource-allocation processes to evaluate disruptive technologies. By almost-any measure, Seagate, based in Scotts Valley, California, was one of the most successful and aggressively managed companies in the history of the microelectronics industry: from its inception in 1980, Seagate's revenues had grown to more than $700 million by 1986. It had pioneered 5.25-inch hard-disk drives and was the main supplier of them to IBM and IBM-compatible personal-computer manufacturers. The company was the leading manufacturer of 5.25-inch drives at the time the disruptive 3.5-inch drives emerged in the mid-1980s.

Engineers at Seagate were the second in the industry to develop working prototypes of 3.5-inch drives. By early 1985, they had made more than 80 such models with a low level of company funding. The engineers forwarded the new models to key marketing executives, and the trade press reported that Seagate was actively developing 3.5-inch drives. But Seagate's principal customers—IBM and other manufacturers of AT-class personal computers—showed no interest in the new drives. They wanted to incorporate 40-MB and 60-MB drives in their next-generation models, and Seagate's early 3.5-inch prototypes packed only 10 MB. In response, Seagate's marketing executives lowered their sales forecasts for the new disk drives.

Manufacturing and financial executives at the company pointed out another drawback to the 3.5-inch drives. According to their analysis, the new drives would never be competitive with the 5.25-inch architecture on a cost-permegabyte basis—an important metric that Seagate's customers used to evaluate disk drives. Given Seagate's cost structure, margins on the higher-capacity 5.25-inch models therefore promised to be much higher than those on the smaller products.

Senior managers quite rationally decided that the 3.5-inch drive would not provide the sales volume and profit margins that Seagate needed from a new product. A former Seagate marketing executive recalled, "We needed a new model that could become the next ST412 [a 5.25-inch drive generating more than $300 million in annual sales, which was nearing the end of its life cycle]. At the time, the entire market for 3.5-inch drives was less than $50 million. The 3.5-inch drive just didn't fit the bill—for sales or profits."

The shelving of the 3.5-inch drive was *not* a signal that Seagate was complacent about innovation. Seagate subsequently introduced new models of 5.25-inch drives at an accelerated rate and, in so doing, introduced an impressive array of sustaining technological improvements, even though introducing them rendered a significant portion of its manufacturing capacity obsolete.

While Seagate's attention was glued to the personal-computer market, former employees of Seagate and other 5.25-inch drive makers, who had become frustrated by their employers' delays in launching 3.5-inch drives, founded a new company, Conner Peripherals. Conner focused on selling its 3.5-inch drives to companies in emerging markets for portable computers and small-footprint desktop products (PCs that take up a smaller amount of space on a desk). Conner's primary customer was Compaq Computer, a customer that Seagate had never served. Seagate's own prosperity, coupled with Conner's focus on customers who valued different disk-drive attributes (ruggedness, physical volume, and weight), minimized the threat Seagate saw in Conner and its 3.5-inch drives.

From its beachhead in the emerging market for portable computers, however, Conner improved the storage capacity of its drives by

50% per year. By the end of 1987, 3.5-inch drives packed the capacity demanded in the mainstream personal-computer market. At this point, Seagate executives took their company's 3.5-inch drive off the shelf, introducing it to the market as a *defensive* response to the attack of entrant companies like Conner and Quantum Corporation, the other pioneer of 3.5-inch drives. But it was too late.

By then, Seagate faced strong competition. For a while, the company was able to defend its existing market by selling 3.5-inch drives to its established customer base—manufacturers and resellers of full-size personal computers. In fact, a large proportion of its 3.5-inch products continued to be shipped in frames that enabled its customers to mount the drives in computers designed to accommodate 5.25-inch drives. But, in the end, Seagate could only struggle to become a second-tier supplier in the new portable-computer market.

In contrast, Conner and Quantum built a dominant position in the new portable-computer market and then used their scale and experience base in designing and manufacturing 3.5-inch products to drive Seagate from the personal-computer market. In their 1994 fiscal years, the combined revenues of Conner and Quantum exceeded $5 billion.

Seagate's poor timing typifies the responses of many established companies to the emergence of disruptive technologies. Seagate was willing to enter the market for 3.5-inch drives only when it had become large enough to satisfy the company's financial requirements—that is, only when existing customers wanted the new technology. Seagate has survived through its savvy acquisition of Control Data Corporation's disk-drive business in 1990. With CDC's technology base and Seagate's volume-manufacturing expertise, the company has become a powerful player in the business of supplying large-capacity drives for high-end computers. Nonetheless, Seagate has been reduced to a shadow of its former self in the personal-computer market.

It should come as no surprise that few companies, when confronted with disruptive technologies, have been able to overcome the handicaps of size or success. But it can be done. There is a method to spotting and cultivating disruptive technologies.

Determine whether the technology is disruptive or sustaining. The first step is to decide which of the myriad technologies on the horizon are disruptive and, of those, which are real threats. Most companies have well-conceived processes for identifying and tracking the progress of potentially sustaining technologies, because they are important to serving and protecting current customers. But few have systematic processes in place to identify and track potentially disruptive technologies.

One approach to identifying disruptive technologies is to examine internal disagreements over the development of new products or technologies. Who supports the project and who doesn't? Marketing and financial managers, because of their managerial and financial incentives, will rarely support a disruptive technology. On the other hand, technical personnel with outstanding track records will often persist in arguing that a new market for the technology will emerge—even in the face of opposition from key customers and marketing and financial staff. Disagreement between the two groups often signals a disruptive technology that top-level managers should explore.

Define the strategic significance of the disruptive technology. The next step is to ask the right people the right questions about the strategic importance of the disruptive technology. Disruptive technologies tend to stall early in strategic reviews because managers either ask the wrong questions or ask the wrong people the right questions. For example, established companies have regular procedures for asking mainstream customers—especially the important accounts where new ideas are actually tested—to assess the value of innovative products. Generally, these customers are selected because they are the ones striving the hardest to stay ahead of *their* competitors in pushing the performance of *their* products. Hence these customers are most likely to demand the highest performance from their suppliers. For this reason, lead customers are reliably accurate when it comes to assessing the potential of sustaining technologies, but they are reliably *in*accurate when it comes to assessing the potential of disruptive technologies. They are the wrong people to ask.

How to assess disruptive technologies

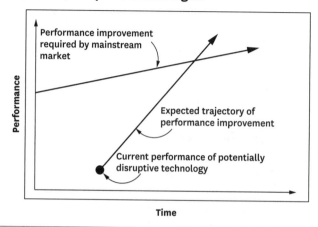

Performance improvement required by mainstream market

Expected trajectory of performance improvement

Current performance of potentially disruptive technology

Performance

Time

A simple graph plotting product performance as it is defined in mainstream markets on the vertical axis and time on the horizontal axis can help managers identify both the right questions and the right people to ask. First, draw a line depicting the level of performance and the trajectory of performance improvement that customers have historically enjoyed and are likely to expect in the future. Then locate the estimated initial performance level of the new technology. If the technology is disruptive, the point will lie far below the performance demanded by current customers. (See the graph "How to assess disruptive technologies.")

What is the likely slope of performance improvement of the disruptive technology compared with the slope of performance improvement demanded by existing markets? If knowledgeable technologists believe the new technology might progress faster than the market's demand for performance improvement, then that technology, which does not meet customers' needs today, may very well address them tomorrow. The new technology, therefore, is strategically critical.

Instead of taking this approach, most managers ask the wrong questions. They compare the anticipated rate of performance improvement of the new technology with that of the established technology. If the new technology has the potential to surpass the established one, the reasoning goes, they should get busy developing it.

Pretty simple. But this sort of comparison, while valid for sustaining technologies, misses the central strategic issue in assessing potentially disruptive technologies. Many of the disruptive technologies we studied *never* surpassed the capability of the old technology. It is the trajectory of the disruptive technology compared with that of the *market* that is significant. For example, the reason the mainframe-computer market is shrinking is not that personal computers outperform mainframes but because personal computers networked with a file server meet the computing and data-storage needs of many organizations effectively. Main-frame-computer makers are reeling not because the performance of personal-computing technology surpassed the performance of mainframe *technology* but because it intersected with the performance demanded by the established *market*.

Consider the graph again. If technologists believe that the new technology will progress at the same rate as the market's demand for performance improvement, the disruptive technology may be slower to invade established markets. Recall that Seagate had targeted personal computing, where demand for hard-disk capacity per computer was growing at 30% per year. Because the capacity of 3.5-inch drives improved at a much faster rate, leading 3.5-inch-drive makers were able to force Seagate out of the market. However, two other 5.25-inch-drive makers, Maxtor and Micropolis, had targeted the engineering-workstation market, in which demand for hard-disk capacity was insatiable. In that market, the trajectory of capacity demanded was essentially parallel to the trajectory of capacity improvement that technologists could supply in the 3.5-inch architecture. As a result, entering the 3.5-inch-drive business was strategically less critical for those companies than it was for Seagate.

Locate the initial market for the disruptive technology. Once managers have determined that a new technology is disruptive and strategically critical, the next step is to locate the initial markets for that technology. Market research, the tool that managers have traditionally relied on, is seldom helpful: at the point a company needs to make a strategic commitment to a disruptive technology, no concrete market exists. When Edwin Land asked Polaroid's market researchers to assess the potential sales of his new camera, they concluded that Polaroid would sell a mere 100,000 cameras over the product's lifetime; few people they interviewed could imagine the uses of instant photography.

Because disruptive technologies frequently signal the emergence of new markets or market segments, managers must *create* information about such markets—who the customers will be, which dimensions of product performance will matter most to which customers, what the right price points will be. Managers can create this kind of information only by experimenting rapidly, iteratively, and inexpensively with both the product and the market.

For established companies to undertake such experiments is very difficult. The resource-allocation processes that are critical to profitability and competitiveness will not—and should not—direct resources to markets in which sales will be relatively small. How, then, can an established company probe a market for a disruptive technology? Let start-ups—either ones the company funds or others with no connection to the company—conduct the experiments. Small, hungry organizations are good at placing economical bets, rolling with the punches, and agilely changing product and market strategies in response to feedback from initial forays into the market.

Consider Apple Computer in its start-up days. The company's original product, the Apple I, was a flop when it was launched in 1977. But Apple had not placed a huge bet on the product and had gotten at least *something* into the hands of early users quickly. The company learned a lot from the Apple I about the new technology and about what customers wanted and did not want. Just as important, a group of *customers* learned about what they did and did not want from personal computers. Armed with this information, Apple launched the Apple II quite successfully.

Many companies could have learned the same valuable lessons by watching Apple closely. In fact, some companies pursue an explicit strategy of being *second to invent*—allowing small pioneers to lead the way into uncharted market territory. For instance, IBM let Apple, Commodore, and Tandy define the personal computer. It then aggressively entered the market and built a considerable personal-computer business.

But IBM's relative success in entering a new market late is the exception, not the rule. All too often, successful companies hold the performance of small-market pioneers to the financial standards they apply to their own performance. In an attempt to ensure that they are using their resources well, companies explicitly or implicitly set relatively high thresholds for the size of the markets they should consider entering. This approach sentences them to making late entries into markets already filled with powerful players.

For example, when the 3.5-inch drive emerged, Seagate needed a $300-million-a-year product to replace its mature flagship 5.25-inch model, the ST412, and the 3.5-inch market wasn't large enough. Over the next two years, when the trade press asked when Seagate would introduce its 3.5-inch drive, company executives consistently responded that there was no market yet. There actually *was* a market, and it was growing rapidly. The signals that Seagate was picking up about the market, influenced as they were by customers who didn't want 3.5-inch drives, were misleading. When Seagate finally introduced its 3.5-inch drive in 1987, more than $750 million in 3.5-inch drives had already been sold. Information about the market's size had been widely available throughout the industry. But it wasn't compelling enough to shift the focus of Seagate's managers. They continued to look at the new market through the eyes of their current customers and in the context of their current financial structure.

The posture of today's leading disk-drive makers toward the newest disruptive technology, 1.8-inch drives, is eerily familiar. Each of the industry leaders has designed one or more models of the tiny drives, and the models are sitting on shelves. Their capacity is too low to be used in notebook computers, and no one yet knows where the initial market for 1.8-inch drives will be. Fax machines, printers, and automobile dashboard mapping systems are all candidates. "There just isn't a market," complained one industry executive. "We've got the product, and the sales force can take orders for it. But there are no orders because nobody needs it. It just sits there." This executive has not considered the fact that his sales force has no incentive to sell the 1.8-inch drives instead of the higher-margin products it sells to higher-volume customers. And while the 1.8-inch drive is sitting on the shelf at his company and others, last year more than $50 million worth of 1.8-inch drives were sold, almost all by startups. This year, the market will be an estimated $150 million.

To avoid allowing small, pioneering companies to dominate new markets, executives must personally monitor the available intelligence on the progress of pioneering companies through monthly meetings with technologists, academics, venture capitalists, and other nontraditional sources of information. They *cannot* rely on the company's traditional channels for gauging markets because those channels were not designed for that purpose.

Place responsibility for building a disruptive-technology business in an independent organization. The strategy of forming small teams into skunk-works projects to isolate them from the stifling demands of mainstream organizations is widely known but poorly understood. For example, isolating a team of engineers so that it can develop a radically new sustaining technology just because that technology is radically different is a fundamental misapplication of the skunk-works approach. Managing out of context is also unnecessary in the unusual event that a disruptive technology is more financially attractive than existing products. Consider Intel's transition from dynamic random access memory (DRAM) chips to microprocessors. Intel's early microprocessor business had a higher gross margin than that of its DRAM business; in other words, Intel's normal resource-allocation process naturally provided the new business with the resources it needed.[1]

Creating a separate organization is necessary only when the disruptive technology has a lower profit margin than the mainstream business and must serve the unique needs of a new set of customers. CDC, for example, successfully created a remote organization to commercialize its 5.25-inch drive. Through 1980, CDC was the dominant independent disk-drive supplier due to its expertise in making 14-inch drives for mainframe-computer makers. When the 8-inch drive emerged, CDC launched a late development effort, but its engineers were repeatedly pulled off the project to solve problems for the more profitable, higher-priority 14-inch projects targeted at the company's most important customers. As a result, CDC was three years late in launching its first 8-inch product and never captured more than 5% of that market.

When the 5.25-inch generation arrived, CDC decided that it would face the new challenge more strategically. The company assigned a small group of engineers and marketers in Oklahoma City, Oklahoma, far from the mainstream organization's customers, the task of developing and commercializing a competitive 5.25-inch product. "We needed to launch it in an environment in which everybody got excited about a $50,000 order," one executive recalled. "In Minneapolis, you needed a $1 million order to turn anyone's head." CDC never regained the 70% share it had once enjoyed in the market for mainframe disk drives, but its Oklahoma City operation secured a profitable 20% of the high-performance 5.25-inch market.

Had Apple created a similar organization to develop its Newton personal digital assistant (PDA), those who have pronounced it a flop might have deemed it a success. In launching the product, Apple made the mistake of acting as if it were dealing with an established market. Apple managers went into the PDA project assuming that it had to make a significant contribution to corporate growth. Accordingly, they researched customer desires exhaustively and then bet huge sums launching the Newton. Had Apple made a more modest technological and financial bet and entrusted the Newton to an organization the size that Apple itself was when it launched the Apple I, the outcome might have been different. The Newton might have been seen more broadly as a solid step forward in the quest to discover what customers really want. In fact, many more Newtons than Apple I models were sold within a year of their introduction.

Keep the disruptive organization independent. Established companies can only dominate emerging markets by creating small organizations of the sort CDC created in Oklahoma City. But what should they do when the emerging market becomes large and established?

Most managers assume that once a spin-off has become commercially viable in a new market, it should be integrated into the mainstream organization. They reason that the fixed costs associated with engineering, manufacturing, sales, and distribution activities can be shared across a broader group of customers and products.

This approach might work with sustaining technologies; however, with disruptive technologies, folding the spin-off into the mainstream organization can be disastrous. When the independent and mainstream organizations are folded together in order to share resources, debilitating arguments inevitably arise over which groups get what resources and whether or when to cannibalize established products. In the history of the disk-drive industry, every company that has tried to manage main-stream and disruptive businesses within a single organization failed.

No matter the industry, a corporation consists of business units with finite life spans: the technological and market bases of any business will eventually disappear. Disruptive technologies are part of that cycle. Companies that understand this process can create new businesses to replace the ones that must inevitably die. To do so, companies must give managers of disruptive innovation free rein to realize the technology's full potential—even if it means ultimately killing the mainstream business. For the corporation to live, it must be willing to see business units die. If the corporation doesn't kill them off itself, competitors will.

The key to prospering at points of disruptive change is not simply to take more risks, invest for the long term, or fight bureaucracy. The key is to manage strategically important disruptive technologies in an organizational context where small orders create energy, where fast low-cost forays into ill-defined markets are possible, and where overhead is low enough to permit profit even in emerging markets.

Managers of established companies can master disruptive technologies with extraordinary success. But when they seek to develop and launch a disruptive technology that is rejected by important customers within the context of the mainstream business's financial demands, they fail—not because they make the wrong decisions, but because they make the right decisions for circumstances that are about to become history.

Originally published in January–February 1995. Reprint 95103

Note

1. Robert A. Burgelman, "Fading Memories: A Process Theory of Strategic Business Exit in Dynamic Environments," *Administrative Science Quarterly* 39 (1994), pp. 24–56.

Meeting the Challenge of Disruptive Change

by Clayton M. Christensen and Michael Overdorf

THESE ARE SCARY TIMES for managers in big companies. Even before the Internet and globalization, their track record for dealing with major, disruptive change was not good. Out of hundreds of department stores, for example, only one—Dayton Hudson—became a leader in discount retailing. Not one of the minicomputer companies succeeded in the personal-computer business. Medical and business schools are struggling—and failing—to change their curricula fast enough to train the types of doctors and managers their markets need. The list could go on.

It's not that managers in big companies can't see disruptive changes coming. Usually they can. Nor do they lack resources to confront them. Most big companies have talented managers and specialists, strong product portfolios, first-rate technological know-how, and deep pockets. What managers lack is a habit of thinking about their organization's capabilities as carefully as they think about individual people's capabilities.

One of the hallmarks of a great manager is the ability to identify the right person for the right job and to train employees to succeed at the jobs they're given. But unfortunately, most managers assume that if each person working on a project is well matched to the job, then the organization in which they work will be, too. Often that is not the case. One could put two sets of identically capable people to work in different organizations, and what they accomplished would be significantly different. That's because organizations themselves—independent of the people and other resources in them—have capabilities. To succeed consistently, good managers need to be skilled not just in assessing people but also in assessing the abilities and disabilities of their organization as a whole.

This article offers managers a framework to help them understand what their organizations are capable of accomplishing. It will show them how their company's disabilities become more sharply defined even as its core capabilities grow. It will give them a way to recognize different kinds of change and make appropriate organizational responses to the opportunities that arise from each. And it will offer some bottom-line advice that runs counter to much that's assumed in our can-do business culture: if an organization faces major change—a disruptive innovation, perhaps—the worst possible approach may be to make drastic adjustments to the existing organization. In trying to transform an enterprise, managers can destroy the very capabilities that sustain it.

Before rushing into the breach, managers must understand precisely what types of change the existing organization is capable and incapable of handling. To help them do that, we'll first take a systematic look at how to recognize a company's core capabilities on an organizational level and then examine how those capabilities migrate as companies grow and mature.

Where Capabilities Reside

Our research suggests that three factors affect what an organization can and cannot do: its resources, its processes, and its values. When thinking about what sorts of innovations their organization will be able to embrace, managers need to assess how each of these factors might affect their organization's capacity to change.

Idea in Brief

Why do so few established companies innovate successfully? Of hundreds of department stores, for instance, only Dayton Hudson became a discount-retailing leader. And not one minicomputer company succeeded in the personal-computer business.

What's going on? After all, most established firms boast deep pockets and talented people. But when a new venture captures their imagination, they get their people working on it within organizational structures (such as functional teams) designed to surmount *old* challenges—not ones that the new venture is facing.

To avoid this mistake, ask:

- **"Does my organization have the right *resources* to support this innovation?"** Resources supporting business-as-usual—people, technologies, product designs, brands, customer and supplier relationships—rarely match those required for new ventures.

- **"Does my organization have the right *processes* to innovate?"** Processes supporting your established business—decision-making protocols, coordination patterns—may hamstring your new venture.

- **"Does my organization have the right *values* to innovate?"** Consider how you decide whether to commit to a new venture. For example, can you tolerate lower profit margins than your established enterprise demands?

- **"What team and structure will best support our innovation effort?"** Should you use a team dedicated to the project within your company? Create a separate spin-off organization?

By selecting the right team and organizational structure for your innovation—and infusing it with the right resources, processes, and values—you heighten your chances of innovating successfully.

Resources

When they ask the question, "What can this company do?" the place most managers look for the answer is in its resources—both the tangible ones like people, equipment, technologies, and cash, and the less tangible ones like product designs, information, brands, and relationships with suppliers, distributors, and customers. Without doubt, access to abundant, high-quality resources increases an organization's chances of coping with change. But resource analysis doesn't come close to telling the whole story.

Idea in Practice

Selecting the Right Structure for Your Innovation

If your innovation . . .	Select this type of team . . .	To operate . . .	Because . . .
Fits *well* with your existing values *and* processes	**Functional teams** who work sequentially on issues, or **lightweight teams**—ad hoc cross-functional teams who work simultaneously on multiple issues	Within your existing organization	Owing to the good fit with existing processes and values, no new capabilities or organizational structures are called for.
Fits *well* with existing values but *poorly* with existing processes	**Heavyweight team** dedicated exclusively to the innovation project, with complete responsibility for its success	Within your existing organization	The poor fit with existing processes requires new types of coordination among groups and individuals.
Fits *poorly* with existing values but *well* with existing processes	**Heavyweight team** dedicated exclusively to the innovation project, with complete responsibility for its success	Within your existing organization for development, followed by a spin-off for commercialization	In-house development capitalizes on existing processes. A spin-off for the commercialization phase facilitates new values—such as a different cost structure with lower profit margins.
Fits *poorly* with your existing processes *and* values	**Heavyweight team** dedicated exclusively to the innovation project, with complete responsibility for its success	In a separate spin-off or acquired organization	A spin-off enables the project to be governed by different values *and* ensures that new processes emerge.

Processes

The second factor that affects what a company can and cannot do is its processes. By processes, we mean the patterns of interaction, coordination, communication, and decision making employees use to transform resources into products and services of greater worth. Such examples as the processes that govern product development, manufacturing, and budgeting come immediately to mind. Some processes are formal, in the sense that they are explicitly defined and documented. Others are informal: they are routines or ways of working that evolve over time. The former tend to be more visible, the latter less visible.

One of the dilemmas of management is that processes, by their very nature, are set up so that employees perform tasks in a consistent way, time after time. They are *meant* not to change or, if they must change, to change through tightly controlled procedures. When people use a process to do the task it was designed for, it is likely to perform efficiently. But when the same process is used to tackle a very different task, it is likely to perform sluggishly. Companies focused on developing and winning FDA approval for new drug compounds, for example, often prove inept at developing and winning approval for medical devices because the second task entails very different ways of working. In fact, a process that creates the capability to execute one task concurrently defines disabilities in executing other tasks.[1]

The most important capabilities and concurrent disabilities aren't necessarily embodied in the most visible processes, like logistics, development, manufacturing, or customer service. In fact, they are more likely to be in the less visible, background processes that support decisions about where to invest resources—those that define how market research is habitually done, how such analysis is translated into financial projections, how plans and budgets are negotiated internally, and so on. It is in those processes that many organizations' most serious disabilities in coping with change reside.

Values

The third factor that affects what an organization can and cannot do is its values. Sometimes the phrase "corporate values" carries an ethical connotation: one thinks of the principles that ensure patient well-being for Johnson & Johnson or that guide decisions about employee safety at Alcoa. But within our framework, "values" has a broader meaning. We define an organization's values as the standards by which employees set priorities that enable them to judge whether an order is attractive or unattractive, whether a customer is more important or less important, whether an idea for a new product is attractive or marginal, and so on. Prioritization decisions are made by employees at every level. Among salespeople, they consist of on-the-spot, day-to-day decisions about which products to push with customers and which to de-emphasize. At the executive tiers, they often take the form of decisions to invest, or not, in new products, services, and processes.

The larger and more complex a company becomes, the more important it is for senior managers to train employees throughout the organization to make independent decisions about priorities that are consistent with the strategic direction and the business model of the company. A key metric of good management, in fact, is whether such clear, consistent values have permeated the organization.

But consistent, broadly understood values also define what an organization cannot do. A company's values reflect its cost structure or its business model because those define the rules its employees must follow for the company to prosper. If, for example, a company's overhead costs require it to achieve gross profit margins of 40%, then a value or decision rule will have evolved that encourages middle managers to kill ideas that promise gross margins below 40%. Such an organization would be incapable of commercializing projects targeting low-margin markets—such as those in e-commerce—even though another organization's values, driven by a very different cost structure, might facilitate the success of the same project.

Different companies, of course, embody different values. But we want to focus on two sets of values in particular that tend to evolve in most companies in very predictable ways. The inexorable evolution of these two values is what makes companies progressively less capable of addressing disruptive change successfully.

As in the previous example, the first value dictates the way the company judges acceptable gross margins. As companies add features and functions to their products and services, trying to capture more attractive customers in premium tiers of their markets, they often add overhead cost. As a result, gross margins that were once attractive become unattractive. For instance, Toyota entered the North American market with the Corona model, which targeted the lower end of the market. As that segment became crowded with look-alike models from Honda, Mazda, and Nissan, competition drove down profit margins. To improve its margins, Toyota then developed more sophisticated cars targeted at higher tiers. The process of developing cars like the Camry and the Lexus added costs to Toyota's operation. It subsequently decided to exit the lower end of the market; the margins had become unacceptable because the company's cost structure, and consequently its values, had changed.

In a departure from that pattern, Toyota recently introduced the Echo model, hoping to rejoin the entry-level tier with a $10,000 car. It is one thing for Toyota's senior management to decide to launch this new model. It's another for the many people in the Toyota system—including its dealers—to agree that selling more cars at lower margins is a better way to boost profits and equity values than selling more Camrys, Avalons, and Lexuses. Only time will tell whether Toyota can manage this down-market move. To be successful with the Echo, Toyota's management will have to swim against a very strong current—the current of its own corporate values.

The second value relates to how big a business opportunity has to be before it can be interesting. Because a company's stock price represents the discounted present value of its projected earnings stream, most managers feel compelled not just to maintain growth but to maintain a constant rate of growth. For a $40 million company to grow 25%, for instance, it needs to find $10 million in new business the next year. But a $40 billion company needs to find $10 billion in new business the next year to grow at that same rate. It follows that an opportunity that excites a small company isn't big enough to be interesting to a large company. One of the bitter-sweet results of success, in fact, is that as companies become large, they lose the ability to enter small, emerging markets. This disability is not caused by a change in the resources within the companies—their resources typically are vast. Rather, it's caused by an evolution in values.

The problem is magnified when companies suddenly become much bigger through mergers or acquisitions. Executives and Wall Street financiers who engineer megamergers between already-huge pharmaceutical companies, for example, need to take this effect into account. Although their merged research organizations might have more resources to throw at new product development, their commercial organizations will probably have lost their appetites for all but the biggest blockbuster drugs. This constitutes a very real disability in managing innovation. The same problem crops up in high-tech industries as well. In many ways, Hewlett-Packard's recent decision to split itself into two companies is rooted in its recognition of this problem.

The Migration of Capabilities

In the start-up stages of an organization, much of what gets done is attributable to resources—people, in particular. The addition or departure of a few key people can profoundly influence its success. Over time, however, the locus of the organization's capabilities shifts toward its processes and values. As people address recurrent tasks, processes become defined. And as the business model takes shape and it becomes clear which types of business need to be accorded highest priority, values coalesce. In fact, one reason that many soaring young companies flame out after an IPO based on a single hot product is that their initial success is grounded in resources—often the founding engineers—and they fail to develop processes that can create a sequence of hot products.

Avid Technology, a producer of digital-editing systems for television, is an apt case in point. Avid's well-received technology removed tedium from the video-editing process. On the back of its star product, Avid's stock rose from $16 a share at its 1993 IPO to $49 in mid-1995. However, the strains of being a one-trick pony soon emerged as Avid faced a saturated market, rising inventories and receivables, increased competition, and shareholder lawsuits. Customers loved the product, but Avid's lack of effective processes for consistently developing new products and for controlling quality, delivery, and service ultimately tripped the company and sent its stock back down.

By contrast, at highly successful firms such as McKinsey & Company, the processes and values have become so powerful that it almost doesn't matter which people get assigned to which project teams. Hundreds of MBAs join the firm every year, and almost as many leave. But the company is able to crank out high-quality work year after year because its core capabilities are rooted in its processes and values rather than in its resources.

When a company's processes and values are being formed in its early and middle years, the founder typically has a profound impact. The founder usually has strong opinions about how employees should do their work and what the organization's priorities need to be. If the founder's judgments are flawed, of course, the company will likely fail. But if they're sound, employees will experience for themselves the validity of the founder's problem-solving and decision-making methods. Thus processes become defined. Likewise, if the company becomes financially successful by allocating resources according to criteria that reflect the founder's priorities, the company's values coalesce around those criteria.

As successful companies mature, employees gradually come to assume that the processes and priorities they've used so successfully so often are the right way to do their work. Once that happens and employees begin to follow processes and decide priorities by assumption rather than by conscious choice, those processes and values come to constitute the organization's culture.[2] As companies grow from a few employees to hundreds and thousands of them, the

Digital's Dilemma

A LOT OF BUSINESS THINKERS have analyzed Digital Equipment Corporation's abrupt fall from grace. Most have concluded that Digital simply read the market very badly. But if we look at the company's fate through the lens of our framework, a different picture emerges.

Digital was a spectacularly successful maker of minicomputers from the 1960s through the 1980s. One might have been tempted to assert, when personal computers first appeared in the market around 1980, that Digital's core capability was in building computers. But if that were the case, why did the company stumble?

Clearly, Digital had the resources to succeed in personal computers. Its engineers routinely designed computers that were far more sophisticated than PCs. The company had plenty of cash, a great brand, good technology, and so on. But it did not have the processes to succeed in the personal-computer business. Minicomputer companies designed most of the key components of their computers internally and then integrated those components into proprietary configurations. Designing a new product platform took two to three years. Digital manufactured most of its own components and assembled them in a batch mode. It sold directly to corporate engineering organizations. Those processes worked extremely well in the minicomputer business.

PC makers, by contrast, outsourced most components from the best suppliers around the globe. New computer designs, made up of modular components, had to be completed in six to 12 months. The computers were manufactured in high-volume assembly lines and sold through retailers to consumers and businesses. None of these processes existed within Digital. In other words, although the people working at the company had the ability to design, build, and sell personal computers profitably, they were working in an organization that was incapable of doing so because its processes had been designed and had evolved to do other tasks well.

Similarly, because of its overhead costs, Digital had to adopt a set of values that dictated, "If it generates 50% gross margins or more, it's good business. If it generates less than 40% margins, it's not worth doing." Management had to ensure that all employees gave priority to projects according to these criteria or the company couldn't make money. Because PCs generated lower margins, they did not fit with Digital's values. The company's criteria for setting priorities always placed higher-performance minicomputers ahead of personal computers in the resource-allocation process.

Digital could have created a different organization that would have honed the different processes and values required to succeed in PCs—as IBM did. But Digital's mainstream organization simply was incapable of succeeding at the job.

challenge of getting all employees to agree on what needs to be done and how can be daunting for even the best managers. Culture is a powerful management tool in those situations. It enables employees to act autonomously but causes them to act consistently.

Hence, the factors that define an organization's capabilities and disabilities evolve over time—they start in resources; then move to visible, articulated processes and values; and migrate finally to culture. As long as the organization continues to face the same sorts of problems that its processes and values were designed to address, managing the organization can be straightforward. But because those factors also define what an organization cannot do, they constitute disabilities when the problems facing the company change fundamentally. When the organization's capabilities reside primarily in its people, changing capabilities to address the new problems is relatively simple. But when the capabilities have come to reside in processes and values, and especially when they have become embedded in culture, change can be extraordinarily difficult. (See the sidebar "Digital's Dilemma.")

Sustaining versus Disruptive Innovation

Successful companies, no matter what the source of their capabilities, are pretty good at responding to evolutionary changes in their markets—what in *The Innovator's Dilemma* (Harvard Business School, 1997), Clayton Christensen referred to as *sustaining innovation*. Where they run into trouble is in handling or initiating revolutionary changes in their markets, or dealing with *disruptive innovation*.

Sustaining technologies are innovations that make a product or service perform better in ways that customers in the mainstream market already value. Compaq's early adoption of Intel's 32-bit 386 microprocessor instead of the 16-bit 286 chip was a sustaining innovation. So was Merrill Lynch's introduction of its Cash Management Account, which allowed customers to write checks against their equity accounts. Those were breakthrough innovations that sustained the best customers of these companies by providing something better than had previously been available.

Disruptive innovations create an entirely new market through the introduction of a new kind of product or service, one that's actually worse, initially, as judged by the performance metrics that mainstream customers value. Charles Schwab's initial entry as a bare-bones discount broker was a disruptive innovation relative to the offerings of full-service brokers like Merrill Lynch. Merrill Lynch's best customers wanted more than Schwab-like services. Early personal computers were a disruptive innovation relative to mainframes and minicomputers. PCs were not powerful enough to run the computing applications that existed at the time they were introduced. These innovations were disruptive in that they didn't address the next-generation needs of leading customers in existing markets. They had other attributes, of course, that enabled new market applications to emerge—and the disruptive innovations improved so rapidly that they ultimately could address the needs of customers in the mainstream of the market as well.

Sustaining innovations are nearly always developed and introduced by established industry leaders. But those same companies never introduce—or cope well with—disruptive innovations. Why? Our resources-processes-values framework holds the answer. Industry leaders are organized to develop and introduce sustaining technologies. Month after month, year after year, they launch new and improved products to gain an edge over the competition. They do so by developing processes for evaluating the technological potential of sustaining innovations and for assessing their customers' needs for alternatives. Investment in sustaining technology also fits in with the values of leading companies in that they promise higher margins from better products sold to leading-edge customers.

Disruptive innovations occur so intermittently that no company has a routine process for handling them. Furthermore, because disruptive products nearly always promise lower profit margins per unit sold and are not attractive to the company's best customers, they're inconsistent with the established company's values. Merrill Lynch had the resources—the people, money, and technology—required to succeed at the sustaining innovations (Cash Management Account) and the disruptive innovations (bare-bones discount brokering) that it has confronted in recent history. But its processes and values supported only the sustaining innovation: they became disabilities when the company needed to understand and confront the discount and on-line brokerage businesses.

The reason, therefore, that large companies often surrender emerging growth markets is that smaller, disruptive companies are actually more capable of pursuing them. Start-ups lack resources, but that doesn't matter. Their values can embrace small markets, and their cost structures can accommodate low margins. Their market research and resource allocation processes allow managers to proceed intuitively; every decision need not be backed by careful research and analysis. All these advantages add up to the ability to embrace and even initiate disruptive change. But how can a large company develop those capabilities?

Creating Capabilities to Cope with Change

Despite beliefs spawned by popular change-management and reengineering programs, processes are not nearly as flexible or adaptable as resources are—and values are even less so. So whether addressing sustaining or disruptive innovations, when an organization needs new processes and values—because it needs new capabilities—managers must create a new organizational space where those capabilities can be developed. There are three possible ways to do that. Managers can

- create new organizational structures within corporate boundaries in which new processes can be developed,

- spin out an independent organization from the existing organization and develop within it the new processes and values required to solve the new problem,

- acquire a different organization whose processes and values closely match the requirements of the new task.

Creating new capabilities internally

When a company's capabilities reside in its processes, and when new challenges require new processes—that is, when they require different people or groups in a company to interact differently and at a different pace than they habitually have done—managers need to pull the relevant people out of the existing organization and draw a new boundary around a new group. Often, organizational boundaries were first drawn to facilitate the operation of existing processes, and they impede the creation of new processes. New team boundaries facilitate new patterns of working together that ultimately can coalesce as new processes. In *Revolutionizing Product Development* (The Free Press, 1992), Steven Wheelwright and Kim Clark referred to these structures as "heavyweight teams."

These teams are entirely dedicated to the new challenge, team members are physically located together, and each member is charged with assuming personal responsibility for the success of the entire project. At Chrysler, for example, the boundaries of the groups within its product development organization historically had been defined by components—power train, electrical systems, and so on. But to accelerate auto development, Chrysler needed to focus not on components but on automobile platforms—the minivan, small car, Jeep, and truck, for example—so it created heavyweight teams. Although these organizational units aren't as good at focusing on component design, they facilitated the definition of new processes that were much faster and more efficient in integrating various subsystems into new car designs. Companies as diverse as Medtronic for its cardiac pacemakers, IBM for its disk drives, and Eli Lilly for its new blockbuster drug Zyprexa have used heavyweight teams as vehicles for creating new processes so they could develop better products faster.

Creating capabilities through a spinout organization

When the mainstream organization's values would render it incapable of allocating resources to an innovation project, the company should spin it out as a new venture. Large organizations cannot be expected to allocate the critical financial and human resources needed to build a strong position in small, emerging markets. And it is very difficult for a company whose cost structure is tailored to compete in high-end markets to be profitable in low-end markets as well. Spinouts are very much in vogue among managers in old-line companies struggling with the question of how to address the Internet. But that's not always appropriate. When a disruptive innovation requires a different cost structure in order to be profitable and competitive, or when the current size of the opportunity is insignificant relative to the growth needs of the mainstream organization, then—and only then—is a spinout organization required.

Hewlett-Packard's laser-printer division in Boise, Idaho, was hugely successful, enjoying high margins and a reputation for superior product quality. Unfortunately, its ink-jet project, which represented a disruptive innovation, languished inside the mainstream HP printer business. Although the processes for developing the two types of printers were basically the same, there was a difference in values. To thrive in the ink-jet market, HP needed to be comfortable with lower gross margins and a smaller market than its laser printers commanded, and it needed to be willing to embrace relatively lower performance standards. It was not until HP's managers decided to transfer the unit to a separate division in Vancouver, British Columbia, with the goal of competing head-to-head with its own laser business, that the ink-jet business finally became successful.

How separate does such an effort need to be? A new physical location isn't always necessary. The primary requirement is that the project not be forced to compete for resources with projects in the mainstream organization. As we have seen, projects that are inconsistent with a company's mainstream values will naturally be accorded lowest priority. Whether the independent organization is physically separate is less important than its independence from the normal decision-making criteria in the resource allocation process. The sidebar "Fitting the Tool to the Task" goes into more detail about what kind of innovation challenge is best met by which organizational structure.

Managers think that developing a new operation necessarily means abandoning the old one, and they're loathe to do that since it works perfectly well for what it was designed to do. But when disruptive change appears on the horizon, managers need to assemble the capabilities to confront that change before it affects the mainstream business. They actually need to run two businesses in tandem—one

Fitting the Tool to the Task

SUPPOSE THAT AN ORGANIZATION needs to react to or initiate an innovation. The matrix illustrated below can help managers understand what kind of team should work on the project and what organizational structure that team needs to work within. The vertical axis asks the manager to measure the extent to which the organization's existing processes are suited to getting the new job done effectively. The horizontal axis asks managers to assess whether the organization's values will permit the company to allocate the resources the new initiative needs.

In region A, the project is a good fit with the company's processes and values, so no new capabilities are called for. A functional or a lightweight team can tackle the project within the existing organizational structure. A functional team works on function-specific issues, then passes the project on to the next function. A

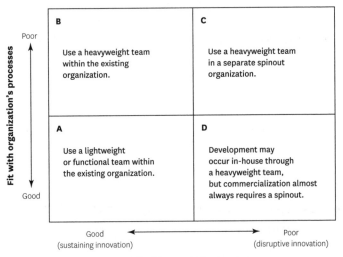

B

Use a heavyweight team within the existing organization.

C

Use a heavyweight team in a separate spinout organization.

A

Use a lightweight or functional team within the existing organization.

D

Development may occur in-house through a heavyweight team, but commercialization almost always requires a spinout.

Poor — Good (vertical axis: Fit with organization's processes)

Good (sustaining innovation) ← → Poor (disruptive innovation)

Fit with organization's values

whose processes are tuned to the existing business model and another that is geared toward the new model. Merrill Lynch, for example, has accomplished an impressive global expansion of its institutional financial services through careful execution of its existing planning, acquisition, and partnership processes. Now, however, faced with the on-line world, the company is required to plan, lightweight team is cross-functional, but team members stay under the control of their respective functional managers.

In region B, the project is a good fit with the company's values but not with its processes. It presents the organization with new types of problems and therefore requires new types of interactions and coordination among groups and individuals. The team, like the team in region A, is working on a sustaining rather than a disruptive innovation. In this case, a heavyweight team is a good bet, but the project can be executed within the mainstream company. A heavyweight team— whose members work solely on the project and are expected to behave like general managers, shouldering responsibility for the project's success—is designed so that new processes and new ways of working together can emerge.

In region C, the manager faces a disruptive change that doesn't fit the organization's existing processes or values. To ensure success, the manager should create a spinout organization and commission a heavyweight development team to tackle the challenge. The spinout will allow the project to be governed by different values—a different cost structure, for example, with lower profit margins. The heavyweight team (as in region B) will ensure that new processes can emerge.

Similarly, in region D, when a manager faces a disruptive change that fits the organization's current processes but doesn't fit its values, the key to success almost always lies in commissioning a heavyweight development team to work in a spinout. Development may occasionally happen successfully in-house, but successful commercialization will require a spinout.

Unfortunately, most companies employ a one-size-fits-all organizing strategy, using lightweight or functional teams for programs of every size and character. But such teams are tools for exploiting established capabilities. And among those few companies that have accepted the heavyweight gospel, many have attempted to organize all of their development teams in a heavyweight fashion. Ideally, each company should tailor the team structure and organizational location to the process and values required by each project.

acquire, and form partnerships more rapidly. Does that mean Merrill Lynch should change the processes that have worked so well in its traditional investment-banking business? Doing so would be disastrous, if we consider the question through the lens of our framework. Instead, Merrill should retain the old processes when working with the existing business (there are probably a few billion dollars still to be made under the old business model!) and create additional processes to deal with the new class of problems.

One word of warning: in our studies of this challenge, we have never seen a company succeed in addressing a change that disrupts its mainstream values without the personal, attentive oversight of the CEO—precisely because of the power of values in shaping the normal resource allocation process. Only the CEO can ensure that the new organization gets the required resources and is free to create processes and values that are appropriate to the new challenge. CEOs who view spinouts as a tool to get disruptive threats off their personal agendas are almost certain to meet with failure. We have seen no exceptions to this rule.

Creating capabilities through acquisitions

Just as innovating managers need to make separate assessments of the capabilities and disabilities that reside in their company's resources, processes, and values, so must they do the same with acquisitions when seeking to buy capabilities. Companies that successfully gain new capabilities through acquisitions are those that know where those capabilities reside in the acquisition and assimilate them accordingly. Acquiring managers begin by asking, "What created the value that I just paid so dearly for? Did I justify the price because of the acquisition's resources? Or was a substantial portion of its worth created by processes and values?"

If the capabilities being purchased are embedded in an acquired company's processes and values, then the last thing the acquiring manager should do is integrate the acquisition into the parent organization. Integration will vaporize the processes and values of the acquired firm. Once the acquisition's managers are forced to adopt the buyer's way of doing business, its capabilities will disappear. A better strategy is to let the business stand alone and to infuse the parent's resources into the acquired company's processes and values. This approach truly constitutes the acquisition of new capabilities.

If, however, the acquired company's resources were the reason for its success and the primary rationale for the acquisition, then integrating it into the parent can make a lot of sense. Essentially, that means plugging the acquired people, products, technology, and customers into the parent's processes as a way of leveraging the parent's existing capabilities.

The perils of the ongoing DaimlerChrysler merger can be better understood in this light. Chrysler had few resources that could be considered unique. Its recent success in the market was rooted in its processes—particularly in its processes for designing products and integrating the efforts of its subsystem suppliers. What is the best way for Daimler to leverage Chrysler's capabilities? Wall Street is pressuring management to consolidate the two organizations to cut costs. But if the two companies are integrated, the very processes that made Chrysler such an attractive acquisition will likely be compromised.

The situation is reminiscent of IBM's 1984 acquisition of the telecommunications company Rolm. There wasn't anything in Rolm's pool of resources that IBM didn't already have. Rather, it was Rolm's processes for developing and finding new markets for PBX products that mattered. Initially, IBM recognized the value in preserving the informal and unconventional culture of the Rolm organization, which stood in stark contrast to IBM's methodical style. However, in 1987 IBM terminated Rolm's subsidiary status and decided to fully integrate the company into its own corporate structure. IBM's managers soon learned the folly of that decision. When they tried to push Rolm's resources—its products and its customers—through the processes that had been honed in the large-computer business, the Rolm business stumbled badly. And it was impossible for a computer company whose values had been whetted on profit margins of 18% to get excited about products with much lower profit margins. IBM's integration of Rolm destroyed the very source of the deal's original worth. Daimler-Chrysler, bowing to the investment community's drumbeat for efficiency savings, now stands on the edge of the same precipice. Often, it seems, financial analysts have a better intuition about the value of resources than they do about the value of processes.

By contrast, Cisco Systems' acquisitions process has worked well because, we would argue, it has kept resources, processes, and values in the right perspective. Between 1993 and 1997, it primarily acquired small companies that were less than two years old, early-stage organizations whose market value was built primarily upon their resources, particularly their engineers and products. Cisco plugged those resources into its own effective development, logistics, manufacturing, and marketing processes and threw away whatever nascent processes and values came with the acquisitions because those weren't what it had paid for. On a couple of occasions when the company acquired a larger, more mature organization—notably its 1996 acquisition of StrataCom—Cisco did not integrate. Rather, it let StrataCom stand alone and infused Cisco's substantial resources into StrataCom's organization to help it grow more rapidly.[3]

Managers whose organizations are confronting change must first determine whether they have the resources required to succeed. They then need to ask a separate question: Does the organization have the processes and values it needs to succeed in this new situation? Asking this second question is not as instinctive for most managers because the processes by which work is done and the values by which employees make their decisions have served them well in the past. What we hope this framework introduces into managers' thinking is the idea that the very capabilities that make their organizations effective also define their disabilities. In that regard, a little time spent soul-searching for honest answers to the following questions will pay off handsomely: Are the processes by which work habitually gets done in the organization appropriate for this new problem? And will the values of the organization cause this initiative to get high priority or to languish?

If the answers to those questions are no, it's okay. Understanding a problem is the most crucial step in solving it. Wishful thinking about these issues can set teams that need to innovate on a course fraught with roadblocks, second-guessing, and frustration. The reason that innovation often seems to be so difficult for established companies is that they employ highly capable people and then set them to work within organizational structures whose processes and values weren't designed for the task at hand. Ensuring that capable people are ensconced in capable organizations is a major responsibility of management in a transformational age such as ours.

Originally published in March 2000. Reprint R00202

Notes

1. See Dorothy Leonard-Barton, "Core Capabilities and Core Rigidities: A Paradox in Managing New Product Development," *Strategic Management Journal* (summer, 1992).

2. Our description of the development of an organization's culture draws heavily from Edgar Schein's research, as first laid out in his book *Organizational Culture and Leadership* (Jossey-Bass Publishers, 1985).

3. See Charles A. Holloway, Stephen C. Wheelwright, and Nicole Tempest, "Cisco Systems, Inc.: Post-Acquisition Manufacturing Integration," a case published jointly by the Stanford and Harvard business schools, 1998.

Marketing Malpractice

The Cause and the Cure. *by Clayton M. Christensen, Scott Cook, and Taddy Hall*

THIRTY THOUSAND new consumer products are launched each year. But over 90% of them fail—and that's after marketing professionals have spent massive amounts of money trying to understand what their customers want. What's wrong with this picture? Is it that market researchers aren't smart enough? That advertising agencies aren't creative enough? That consumers have become too difficult to understand? We don't think so. We believe, instead, that some of the fundamental paradigms of marketing—the methods that most of us learned to segment markets, build brands, and understand customers—are broken. We're not alone in that judgment. Even Procter & Gamble CEO A.G. Lafley, arguably the best-positioned person in the world to make this call, says, "We need to reinvent the way we market to consumers. We need a new model."

To build brands that mean something to customers, you need to attach them to products that mean something to customers. And to do that, you need to segment markets in ways that reflect how customers actually live their lives. In this article, we will propose a way to reconfigure the principles of market segmentation. We'll describe how to create products that customers will consistently value. And finally, we will describe how new, valuable brands can be built to truly deliver sustained, profitable growth.

Broken Paradigms of Market Segmentation

The great Harvard marketing professor Theodore Levitt used to tell his students, "People don't want to buy a quarter-inch drill. They want a quarter-inch hole!" Every marketer we know agrees with Levitt's insight. Yet these same people segment their markets by type of drill and by price point; they measure market share of drills, not holes; and they benchmark the features and functions of their drill, not their hole, against those of rivals. They then set to work offering more features and functions in the belief that these will translate into better pricing and market share. When marketers do this, they often solve the wrong problems, improving their products in ways that are irrelevant to their customers' needs.

Segmenting markets by type of customer is no better. Having sliced business clients into small, medium, and large enterprises—or having shoehorned consumers into age, gender, or lifestyle brackets—marketers busy themselves with trying to understand the needs of representative customers in those segments and then create products that address those needs. The problem is that customers don't conform their desires to match those of the average consumer in their demographic segment. When marketers design a product to address the needs of a typical customer in a demographically defined segment, therefore, they cannot know whether any specific individual will buy the product—they can only express a likelihood of purchase in probabilistic terms.

Thus the prevailing methods of segmentation that budding managers learn in business schools and then practice in the marketing departments of good companies are actually a key reason that new product innovation has become a gamble in which the odds of winning are horrifyingly low.

There is a better way to think about market segmentation and new product innovation. The structure of a market, seen from the customers' point of view, is very simple: They just need to get things done, as Ted Levitt said. When people find themselves needing to get a job done, they essentially hire products to do that job for them. The marketer's task is therefore to understand what jobs periodically arise in customers' lives for which they might hire products the company could make.

Idea in Brief

Thirty thousand new consumer products hit store shelves each year. Ninety percent of them fail. Why? We're using misguided market-segmentation practices. For instance, we slice markets based on customer type and define the needs of representative customers in those segments. But actual human beings don't behave like statistically average customers. The consequences? We develop new and enhanced products that don't meet real people's needs.

Here's a better way: Instead of trying to understand the "typical" customer, find out what jobs people want to get done. Then develop **purpose brands:** products or services consumers can "hire" to perform those jobs. FedEx, for example, designed its service to perform the "I-need-to-send-this-from-here-to-there-with-perfect-certainty-as-fast-as-possible" job. FedEx was so much more convenient, reliable, and reasonably priced than the alternatives—the U.S. Postal Service or couriers paid to sit on airlines—that businesspeople around the globe started using "FedEx" as a verb.

A clear purpose brand acts as a two-sided compass: One side guides customers to the right products. The other guides your designers, marketers, and advertisers as they develop and market new and improved products. The payoff? Products your customers consistently value—and brands that deliver sustained profitable growth to your company.

If a marketer can understand the job, design a product and associated experiences in purchase and use to do that job, and deliver it in a way that reinforces its intended use, then when customers find themselves needing to get that job done, they will hire that product.

Since most new-product developers don't think in those terms, they've become much too good at creating products that don't help customers do the jobs they need to get done. Here's an all-too-typical example. In the mid-1990s, Scott Cook presided over the launch of a software product called the Quicken Financial Planner, which helped customers create a retirement plan. It flopped. Though it captured over 90% of retail sales in its product category, annual revenue never surpassed $2 million, and it was eventually pulled from the market.

What happened? Was the $49 price too high? Did the product need to be easier to use? Maybe. A more likely explanation, however, is that while the demographics suggested that lots of families

Idea in Practice

To establish, sustain, and extend your purpose brands:

Observe Consumers in Action

By observing and interviewing people as they're using products, identify jobs they want to get done. Then think of new or enhanced offerings that could do the job better.

Example: A fast-food restaurant wanted to improve milk-shake sales. A researcher watched customers buying shakes, noting that 40% of shakes were purchased by hurried customers early in the morning and carried out to customers' cars. Interviews revealed that most customers bought shakes to do a similar job: make their commute more interesting, stave off hunger until lunchtime, and give them something they could consume

cleanly with one hand. Understanding this job inspired several product-improvement ideas. One example: Move the shake-dispensing machine to the front of the counter and sell customers a prepaid swipe card, so they could dispense shakes themselves and avoid the slow drive-through lane.

Link Products to Jobs through Advertising

Use advertising to clarify the nature of the job your product performs and to give the product a name that reinforces awareness of its purpose. Savvy ads can even help consumers identify needs they weren't consciously aware of before.

Example: Unilever's Asian operations designed a microwavable soup tailored to the job of helping

---

needed a financial plan, constructing one actually wasn't a job that most people were looking to do. The fact that they should have a financial plan, or even that they said they should have a plan, didn't matter. In hindsight, the fact that the design team had had trouble finding enough "planners" to fill a focus group should have tipped Cook off. Making it easier and cheaper for customers to do things that they are not trying to do rarely leads to success.

Designing Products That Do the Job

With few exceptions, every job people need or want to do has a social, a functional, and an emotional dimension. If marketers understand each of these dimensions, then they can design a product that's precisely targeted to the job. In other words, the job, not the office workers boost their energy and productivity in the late afternoon. Called Soupy Snax, the product generated mediocre results. When Unilever renamed it Soupy Snax—4:00 and created ads showing lethargic workers perking up after using the product, ad viewers remarked, "That's what happens to me at 4:00!" Soupy Snax sales soared.

Extend Your Purpose Brand

If you extend your purpose brand onto products that do different jobs—for example, a toothpaste that freshens breath *and* whitens teeth *and* reduces plaque—customers may become confused and lose trust in your brand.

To extend your brand without destroying it:

- **Develop different products that address a common job.** Sony did this with its various generations of Walkman that helped consumers "escape the chaos in my world."

- **Identify new, related jobs and create purpose brands for them.** Marriott International extended its hotel brand, originally built around full-service facilities designed for large meetings, to other types of hotels. Each new purpose brand had a name indicating the job it was designed to do. For instance, Courtyard Marriott was "hired" by individual business travelers seeking a clean, quiet place to get work done in the evening. Residence Inn was hired by longer-term travelers.

customer, is the fundamental unit of analysis for a marketer who hopes to develop products that customers will buy.

To see why, consider one fast-food restaurant's effort to improve sales of its milk shakes. (In this example, both the company and the product have been disguised.) Its marketers first defined the market segment by product—milk shakes—and then segmented it further by profiling the demographic and personality characteristics of those customers who frequently bought milk shakes. Next, they invited people who fit this profile to evaluate whether making the shakes thicker, more chocolaty, cheaper, or chunkier would satisfy them better. The panelists gave clear feedback, but the consequent improvements to the product had no impact on sales.

A new researcher then spent a long day in a restaurant seeking to understand the jobs that customers were trying to get done when they hired a milk shake. He chronicled when each milk shake was bought, what other products the customers purchased, whether these consumers were alone or with a group, whether they consumed the shake on the premises or drove off with it, and so on. He was surprised to find that 40% of all milk shakes were purchased in the early morning. Most often, these early-morning customers were alone; they did not buy anything else; and they consumed their shakes in their cars.

The researcher then returned to interview the morning customers as they left the restaurant, shake in hand, in an effort to understand what caused them to hire a milk shake. Most bought it to do a similar job: They faced a long, boring commute and needed something to make the drive more interesting. They weren't yet hungry but knew that they would be by 10 AM; they wanted to consume something now that would stave off hunger until noon. And they faced constraints: They were in a hurry, they were wearing work clothes, and they had (at most) one free hand.

The researcher inquired further: "Tell me about a time when you were in the same situation but you didn't buy a milk shake. What did you buy instead?" Sometimes, he learned, they bought a bagel. But bagels were too dry. Bagels with cream cheese or jam resulted in sticky fingers and gooey steering wheels. Sometimes these commuters bought a banana, but it didn't last long enough to solve the boring-commute problem. Doughnuts didn't carry people past the 10 AM hunger attack. The milk shake, it turned out, did the job better than any of these competitors. It took people 20 minutes to suck the viscous milk shake through the thin straw, addressing the boring-commute problem. They could consume it cleanly with one hand. By 10:00, they felt less hungry than when they tried the alternatives. It didn't matter much that it wasn't a healthy food, because becoming healthy wasn't essential to the job they were hiring the milk shake to do.

The researcher observed that at other times of the day parents often bought milk shakes, in addition to complete meals, for their children. What job were the parents trying to do? They were exhausted from repeatedly having to say "no" to their kids. They hired milk shakes as an innocuous way to placate their children and feel like loving parents. The researcher observed that the milk shakes didn't do this job very well, though. He saw parents waiting impatiently after they had finished their own meals while their children struggled to suck the thick shakes up through the thin straws.

Customers were hiring milk shakes for two very different jobs. But when marketers had originally asked individual customers who hired a milk shake for either or both jobs which of its attributes they should improve—and when these responses were averaged with those of other customers in the targeted demographic segment—it led to a one-size-fits-none product.

Once they understood the jobs the customers were trying to do, however, it became very clear which improvements to the milk shake would get those jobs done even better and which were irrelevant. How could they tackle the boring-commute job? Make the milk shake even thicker, so it would last longer. And swirl in tiny chunks of fruit, adding a dimension of unpredictability and anticipation to the monotonous morning routine. Just as important, the restaurant chain could deliver the product more effectively by moving the dispensing machine in front of the counter and selling customers a prepaid swipe card so they could dash in, "gas up," and go without getting stuck in the drive-through lane. Addressing the midday and evening job to be done would entail a very different product, of course.

By understanding the job and improving the product's social, functional, and emotional dimensions so that it did the job better, the company's milk shakes would gain share against the real competition—not just competing chains' milk shakes but bananas, boredom, and bagels. This would grow the category, which brings us to an important point: Job-defined markets are generally much larger than product category-defined markets. Marketers who are stuck in the mental trap that equates market size with product categories don't understand whom they are competing against from the customer's point of view.

Notice that knowing how to improve the product did not come from understanding the "typical" customer. It came from understanding the job. Need more evidence?

Pierre Omidyar did not design eBay for the "auction psychographic." He founded it to help people sell personal items. Google was designed for the job of finding information, not for a "search demographic." The unit of analysis in the work that led to Procter & Gamble's stunningly successful Swiffer was the job of cleaning floors, not a demographic or psychographic study of people who mop.

Why do so many marketers try to understand the consumer rather than the job? One reason may be purely historical: In some of the markets in which the tools of modern market research were formulated and tested, such as feminine hygiene or baby care, the job was so closely aligned with the customer demographic that if you understood the customer, you would also understand the job. This coincidence is rare, however. All too frequently, marketers' focus on the customer causes them to target phantom needs.

How a Job Focus Can Grow Product Categories

New growth markets are created when innovating companies design a product and position its brand on a job for which no optimal product yet exists. In fact, companies that historically have segmented and measured the size of their markets by product category generally find that when they instead segment by job, their market is much larger (and their current share of the job is much smaller) than they had thought. This is great news for smart companies hungry for growth.

Understanding and targeting jobs was the key to Sony founder Akio Morita's approach to disruptive innovation. Morita never did conventional market research. Instead, he and his associates spent much of their time watching what people were trying to get done in their lives, then asking themselves whether Sony's electronics miniaturization technology could help them do these things better, easier, and cheaper. Morita would have badly misjudged the size of his market had he simply analyzed trends in the number of tape players being sold before he launched his Walkman. This should trigger an action item on every marketer's to-do list: Turn off the computer, get out of the office, and observe.

Purpose Brands and
Disruptive Innovations

WE HAVE WRITTEN ELSEWHERE about how to harness the potential of disruptive innovations to create growth. Because disruptive innovations are products or services whose performance is not as good as mainstream products, executives of leading companies often hesitate to introduce them for fear of destroying the value of their brands. This fear is generally unfounded, provided that companies attach a unique purpose brand to their disruptive innovations.

Purpose branding has been the key, for example, to Kodak's success with two disruptions. The first was its single-use camera, a classic disruptive technology. Because of its inexpensive plastic lenses, the new camera couldn't take the quality of photographs that a good 35-millimeter camera could produce on Kodak film. The proposition to launch a single-use camera encountered vigorous opposition within Kodak's film division. The corporation finally gave responsibility for the opportunity to a completely different organizational unit, which launched single-use cameras with a purpose brand—the Kodak FunSaver. This was a product customers could hire when they needed to save memories of a fun time but had forgotten to bring a camera or didn't want to risk harming their expensive one. Creating a purpose brand for a disruptive job differentiated the product, clarified its intended use, delighted the customers, and thereby strengthened the endorsing power of the Kodak brand. Quality, after all, can only be measured relative to the job that needs to be done and the alternatives that can be hired to do it. (Sadly, a few years ago, Kodak pushed aside the FunSaver purpose brand in favor of the word "Max," which now appears on its single-use cameras, perhaps to focus on selling film rather than the job the film is for.)

Kodak scored another purpose-branding victory with its disruptive EasyShare digital camera. The company initially had struggled for differentiation and market share in the head-on megapixel and megazoom race against Japanese digital camera makers (all of whom aggressively advertised their corporate brands but had no purpose brands). Kodak then adopted a disruptive strategy that was focused on a job—sharing fun. It made an inexpensive digital camera that customers could slip into a cradle, click "attach" in their computer's e-mail program, and share photos effortlessly with friends and relatives. Sharing fun, not preserving the highest resolution images for posterity, is the job—and Kodak's EasyShare purpose brand guides customers to a product tailored to do that job. Kodak is now the market share leader in digital cameras in the United States.

Consider how Church & Dwight used this strategy to grow its baking soda business. The company has produced Arm & Hammer baking soda since the 1860s; its iconic yellow box and Vulcan's hammer-hefting arm have become enduring visual cues for "the standard of purity." In the late 1960s, market research director Barry Goldblatt tells us, management began observational research to understand the diverse circumstances in which consumers found themselves with a job to do where Arm & Hammer could be hired to help. They found a few consumers adding the product to laundry detergent, a few others mixing it into toothpaste, some sprinkling it on the carpet, and still others placing open boxes in the refrigerator. There was a plethora of jobs out there needing to get done, but most customers did not know that they could hire Arm & Hammer baking soda for these cleaning and freshening jobs. The single product just wasn't giving customers the guidance they needed, given the many jobs it could be hired to do.

Today, a family of job-focused Arm & Hammer products has greatly grown the baking soda product category. These jobs include:

- Help my mouth feel fresh and clean (Arm & Hammer Complete Care toothpaste)

- Deodorize my refrigerator (Arm & Hammer Fridge-n-Freezer baking soda)

- Help my underarms stay clean and fresh (Arm & Hammer Ultra Max deodorant)

- Clean and freshen my carpets (Arm & Hammer Vacuum Free carpet deodorizer)

- Deodorize kitty litter (Arm & Hammer Super Scoop cat litter)

- Make my clothes smell fresh (Arm & Hammer Laundry Detergent).

The yellow-box baking soda business is now less than 10% of Arm & Hammer's consumer revenue. The company's share price has appreciated at nearly four times the average rate of its nearest rivals, P&G,

Unilever, and Colgate-Palmolive. Although the overall Arm & Hammer brand is valuable in each instance, the key to this extraordinary growth is a set of job-focused products and a communication strategy that help people realize that when they find themselves needing to get one of these jobs done, here is a product that they can trust to do it well.

Building Brands That Customers Will Hire

Sometimes, the discovery that one needs to get a job done is conscious, rational, and explicit. At other times, the job is so much a part of a routine that customers aren't really consciously aware of it. Either way, if consumers are lucky, when they discover the job they need to do, a branded product will exist that is perfectly and unambiguously suited to do it. We call the brand of a product that is tightly associated with the job for which it is meant to be hired a *purpose brand*.

The history of Federal Express illustrates how successful purpose brands are built. A job had existed practically forever: the I-need-to-send-this-from-here-to-there-with-perfect-certainty-as-fast-as-possible job. Some U.S. customers hired the U.S. Postal Service's airmail to do this job; a few desperate souls paid couriers to sit on airplanes. Others even went so far as to plan ahead so they could ship via UPS trucks. But each of these alternatives was kludgy, expensive, uncertain, or inconvenient. Because nobody had yet designed a service to do this job well, the brands of the unsatisfactory alternative services became tarnished when they were hired for this purpose. But after Federal Express designed its service to do that exact job, and did it wonderfully again and again, the FedEx brand began popping into people's minds whenever they needed to get that job done. FedEx became a purpose brand—in fact, it became a verb in the international language of business that is inextricably linked with that specific job. It is a very valuable brand as a result.

Most of today's great brands—Crest, Starbucks, Kleenex, eBay, and Kodak, to name a few—started out as just this kind of purpose brand. The product did the job, and customers talked about it. This is how brand equity is built.

Brand equity can be destroyed when marketers don't tie the brand to a purpose. When they seek to build a general brand that does not signal to customers when they should and should not buy the product, marketers run the risk that people might hire their product to do a job it was not designed to do. This causes customers to distrust the brand—as was the case for years with the post office.

A clear purpose brand is like a two-sided compass. One side guides customers to the right products. The other side guides the company's product designers, marketers, and advertisers as they develop and market improved and new versions of their products. A good purpose brand clarifies which features and functions are relevant to the job and which potential improvements will prove irrelevant. The price premium that the brand commands is the wage that customers are willing to pay the brand for providing this guidance on both sides of the compass.

The need to feel a certain way—to feel macho, sassy, pampered, or prestigious—is a job that arises in many of our lives on occasion. When we find ourselves needing to do one of these jobs, we can hire a branded product whose purpose is to provide such feelings. Gucci, Absolut, Montblanc, and Virgin, for example, are purpose brands. They link customers who have one of these jobs to do with experiences in purchase and use that do those jobs well. These might be called aspirational jobs. In some aspirational situations, it is the brand itself, more than the functional dimensions of the product, that gets the job done.

The Role of Advertising

Much advertising is wasted in the mistaken belief that it alone can build brands. Advertising cannot build brands, but it can tell people about an existing branded product's ability to do a job well. That's what the managers at Unilever's Asian operations found out when they identified an important job that arose in the lives of many office workers at around 4:00 in the afternoon. Drained of physical and emotional energy, people still had to get a lot done before their workday ended. They needed something to boost their productivity, and they were hiring a range of caffeinated drinks, candy bars, stretch breaks, and conversation to do this job, with mixed results.

Unilever designed a microwavable soup whose properties were tailored to that job—quick to fix, nutritious but not too filling, it can be consumed at your desk but gives you a bit of a break when you go to heat it up. It was launched into the workplace under the descriptive brand Soupy Snax. The results were mediocre. On a hunch, the brand's managers then relaunched the product with advertisements showing lethargic workers perking up after using the product and renamed the brand Soupy Snax—4:00. The reaction of people who saw the advertisements was, "That's exactly what happens to me at 4:00!" They needed something to help them consciously discover both the job and the product they could hire to do it. The tagline and ads transformed a brand that had been a simple description of a product into a purpose brand that clarified the nature of the job and the product that was designed to do it, and the product has become very successful.

Note the role that advertising played in this process. Advertising clarified the nature of the job and helped more people realize that they had the job to do. It informed people that there was a product designed to do that job and gave the product a name people could remember. Advertising is not a substitute for designing products that do specific jobs and ensuring that improvements in their features and functions are relevant to that job. The fact is that most great brands were built before their owners started advertising. Think of Disney, Harley-Davidson, eBay, and Google. Each brand developed a sterling reputation before much was spent on advertising.

Advertising that attempts to short-circuit this process and build, as if from scratch, a brand that people will trust is a fool's errand. Ford, Nissan, Macy's, and many other companies invest hundreds of millions to keep the corporate name or their products' names in the general consciousness of the buying public. Most of these companies' products aren't designed to do specific jobs and therefore aren't usually differentiated from the competition. These firms have few purpose brands in their portfolios and no apparent strategies to create them. Their managers are unintentionally transferring billions in profits to branding agencies in the vain hope that they can buy their way to glory. What is worse, many companies have decided that building new brands is so expensive they will no longer do so. Brand building by advertising is indeed prohibitively expensive. But that's because it's the wrong way to build a brand.

Marketing mavens are fond of saying that brands are hollow words into which meaning gets stuffed. Beware. Executives who think that brand advertising is an effective mechanism for stuffing meaning into some word they have chosen to be their brand generally succeed in stuffing it full of vagueness. The ad agencies and media companies win big in this game, but the companies whose brands are getting stuffed generally find themselves trapped in an expensive, endless arms race with competitors whose brands are comparably vague.

The exceptions to this brand-building rule are the purpose brands for aspirational jobs, where the brand must be built through images in advertising. The method for brand building that is appropriate for these jobs, however, has been wantonly and wastefully misapplied to the rest of the world of branding.

Extending—Or Destroying—Brand Equity

Once a strong purpose brand has been created, people within the company inevitably want to leverage it by applying it to other products. Executives should consider these proposals carefully. There are rules about the types of extensions that will reinforce the brand—and the types that will erode it.

If a company chooses to extend a brand onto other products that can be hired to do the same job, it can do so without concern that the extension will compromise what the brand does. For example, Sony's portable CD player, although a different product than its original Walkman-branded radio and cassette players, was positioned on the same job (the help-me-escape-the-chaos-in-my-world job). So the new product caused the Walkman brand to pop even more instinctively into customers' minds when they needed to get that job done. Had Sony not been asleep at the switch, a Walkman-branded

MP3 player would have further enhanced this purpose brand. It might even have kept Apple's iPod purpose brand from preempting that job.

The fact that purpose brands are job specific means that when a purpose brand is extended onto products that target different jobs, it will lose its clear meaning as a purpose brand and develop a different character instead—an *endorser brand*. An endorser brand can impart a general sense of quality, and it thereby creates some value in a marketing equation. But general endorser brands lose their ability to guide people who have a particular job to do to products that were designed to do it. Without appropriate guidance, customers will begin using endorser-branded products to do jobs they weren't designed to do. The resulting bad experience will cause customers to distrust the brand. Hence, the value of an endorser brand will erode unless the company adds a second word to its brand architecture—a purpose brand alongside the endorser brand. Different jobs demand different purpose brands.

Marriott International's executives followed this principle when they sought to leverage the Marriott brand to address different jobs for which a hotel might be hired. Marriott had built its hotel brand around full-service facilities that were good to hire for large meetings. When it decided to extend its brand to other types of hotels, it adopted a two-word brand architecture that appended to the Marriott endorsement a purpose brand for each of the different jobs its new hotel chains were intended to do. Hence, individual business travelers who need to hire a clean, quiet place to get work done in the evening can hire Courtyard by Marriott—the hotel designed by business travelers for business travelers. Longer-term travelers can hire Residence Inn by Marriott, and so on. Even though these hotels were not constructed and decorated to the same premium standard as full-service Marriott hotels, the new chains actually reinforce the endorser qualities of the Marriott brand because they do the jobs well that they are hired to do.

Milwaukee Electric Tool has built purpose brands with two—and only two—of the products in its line of power tools. The Milwaukee Sawzall is a reciprocating saw that tradesmen hire when they need to cut through a wall quickly and aren't sure what's under the surface. Plumbers hire Milwaukee's Hole Hawg, a right-angle drill, when they need to drill a hole in a tight space. Competitors like Black & Decker, Bosch, and Makita offer reciprocating saws and right-angle drills with comparable performance and price, but none of them has a purpose brand that pops into a tradesman's mind when he has one of these jobs to do. Milwaukee has owned more than 80% of these two job markets for decades.

Interestingly, Milwaukee offers under its endorser brand a full range of power tools, including circular saws, pistol-grip drills, sanders, and jigsaws. While the durability and relative price of these products are comparable to those of the Sawzall and Hole Hawg, Milwaukee has not built purpose brands for any of these other products. The market share of each is in the low single digits—a testament to the clarifying value of purpose brands versus the general connotation of quality that endorser brands confer. Indeed, a clear purpose brand is usually a more formidable competitive barrier than superior product performance—because competitors can copy performance much more easily than they can copy purpose brands.

The tribulations and successes of P&G's Crest brand is a story of products that ace the customer job, lose their focus, and then bounce back to become strong purpose brands again. Introduced in the mid-1950s, Crest was a classic disruptive technology. Its Fluoristan-reinforced toothpaste made cavity-preventing fluoride treatments cheap and easy to apply at home, replacing an expensive and inconvenient trip to the dentist. Although P&G could have positioned the new product under its existing toothpaste brand, Gleem, its managers chose instead to build a new purpose brand, Crest, which was uniquely positioned on a job. Mothers who wanted to prevent cavities in their children's teeth knew when they saw or heard the word "Crest" that this product was designed to do that job. Because it did the job so well, mothers grew to trust the product and in fact became suspicious of the ability of products without the Crest brand to do that job. This unambiguous association made it a very valuable brand, and Crest passed all its U.S. rivals to become the clear market leader in toothpaste for a generation.

But one cannot sustain victory by standing still. Competitors eventually copied Crest's cavity prevention abilities, turning cavity prevention into a commodity. Crest lost share as competitors innovated in other areas, including flavor, mouthfeel, and commonsense ingredients like baking soda. P&G began copying and advertising these attributes. But unlike Marriott, P&G did not append purpose brands to the general endorsement of Crest, and the brand began losing its distinctiveness.

At the end of the 1990s, new Crest executives brought two disruptions to market, each with its own clear purpose brand. They acquired a start-up named Dr. John's and rebranded its flagship electric toothbrush as the Crest SpinBrush, which they sold for $5—far below the price of competitors' models of the time. They also launched Crest Whitestrips, which allowed people to whiten their teeth at home for a mere $25, far less than dentists charged. With these purpose-branded innovations, Crest generated substantial new growth and regained share leadership in the entire tooth care category.

The exhibit "Extending brands without destroying them" diagrams the two ways marketers can extend a purpose brand without eroding its value. The first option is to move up the vertical axis by developing different products that address a common job. This is what Sony did with its Walkman portable CD player. When Crest was still a clear purpose brand, P&G could have gone this route by, say, introducing a Crest-brand fluoride mouth rinse. The brand would have retained its clarity of purpose. But P&G did not, allowing Johnson & Johnson to insert yet another brand, ACT (its own fluoride mouth rinse), into the cavity-prevention job space. Because P&G pursued the second option, extending its brand along the horizontal axis to other jobs (whitening, breath freshening, and so on), the purpose brand morphed into an endorser brand.

Why Strong Purpose Brands Are So Rare

Given the power that purpose brands have in creating opportunities for differentiation, premium pricing, and growth, isn't it odd that so few companies have a deliberate strategy for creating them?

Extending brands without destroying them

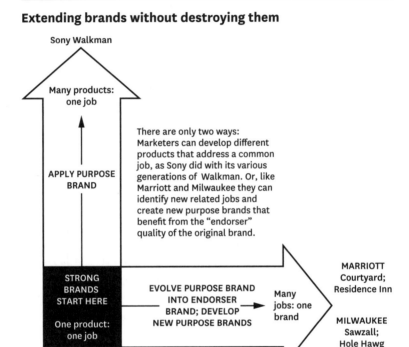

Sony Walkman

Many products:
one job

APPLY PURPOSE
BRAND

There are only two ways:
Marketers can develop different
products that address a common
job, as Sony did with its various
generations of Walkman. Or, like
Marriott and Milwaukee they can
identify new related jobs and
create new purpose brands that
benefit from the "endorser"
quality of the original brand.

STRONG
BRANDS
START HERE

One product:
one job

EVOLVE PURPOSE BRAND
INTO ENDORSER
BRAND; DEVELOP
NEW PURPOSE BRANDS

Many
jobs: one
brand

MARRIOTT
Courtyard;
Residence Inn

MILWAUKEE
Sawzall;
Hole Hawg

Consider the automobile industry. There are a significant number of different jobs that people who purchase cars need to get done, but only a few companies have staked out any of these job markets with purpose brands. Range Rover (until recently, at least) was a clear and valuable purpose brand (the take-me-anywhere-with-total-dependability job). The Volvo brand is positioned on the safety job. Porsche, BMW, Mercedes, Bentley, and Rolls-Royce are associated with various aspirational jobs. The Toyota endorser brand has earned the connotation of reliability. But for so much of the rest? It's hard to know what they mean.

To illustrate: Clayton Christensen recently needed to deliver on a long-promised commitment to buy a car as a college graduation gift for his daughter Annie. There were functional and emotional dimensions to the job. The car needed to be stylish and fun to drive, to be sure. But even more important, as his beloved daughter was venturing off into the cold, cruel world, the big job Clay needed to get done was to know that she was safe and for his sweet Annie to be reminded frequently, as she owned, drove, and serviced the car, that her dad loves and cares for her. A hands-free telephone in the car would be a must, not an option. A version of GM's OnStar service, which called not just the police but Clay in the event of an accident, would be important. A system that reminded the occasionally absentminded Annie when she needed to have the car serviced would take a load off her dad's mind. If that service were delivered as a prepaid gift from her father, it would take another load off Clay's mind because he, too, is occasionally absentminded. Should Clay have hired a Taurus, Escape, Cavalier, Neon, Prizm, Corolla, Camry, Avalon, Sentra, Civic, Accord, Senator, Sonata, or something else? The billions of dollars that automakers spent advertising these brands, seeking somehow to create subtle differentiations in image, helped Clay not at all. Finding the best package to hire was very time-consuming and inconvenient, and the resulting product did the job about as unsatisfactorily as the milk shake had done, a few years earlier.

Focusing a product and its brand on a job creates differentiation. The rub, however, is that when a company communicates the job a branded product was designed to do perfectly, it is also communicating what jobs the product should not be hired to do. Focus is scary—at least the carmakers seem to think so. They deliberately create words as brands that have no meaning in any language, with no tie to any job, in the myopic hope that each individual model will be hired by every customer for every job. The results of this strategy speak for themselves. In the face of compelling evidence that purpose-branded products that do specific jobs well command premium pricing and compete in markets that are much larger than those defined by product categories, the automakers' products are substantially undifferentiated, the average subbrand commands less than a 1% market share, and most automakers are losing money. Somebody gave these folks the wrong recipe for prosperity.

Executives everywhere are charged with generating profitable growth. Rightly, they believe that brands are the vehicles for meeting their growth and profit targets. But success in brand building remains rare. Why? Not for lack of effort or resources. Nor for lack of opportunity in the marketplace. The root problem is that the theories in practice for market segmentation and brand building are riddled with flawed assumptions. Lafley is right. The model is broken. We've tried to illustrate a way out of the death spiral of serial product failure, missed opportunity, and squandered wealth. Marketers who choose to break with the broken past will be rewarded not only with successful brands but with profitably growing businesses as well.

Originally published in December 2005. Reprint 0512D

Innovation Killers

How Financial Tools Destroy Your Capacity to Do New Things. *by Clayton M. Christensen, Stephen P. Kaufman, and Willy C. Shih*

FOR YEARS WE'VE BEEN puzzling about why so many smart, hardworking managers in well-run companies find it impossible to innovate successfully. Our investigations have uncovered a number of culprits, which we've discussed in earlier books and articles. These include paying too much attention to the company's most profitable customers (thereby leaving less-demanding customers at risk) and creating new products that don't help customers do the jobs they want to do. Now we'd like to name the misguided application of three financial-analysis tools as an accomplice in the conspiracy against successful innovation. We allege crimes against these suspects:

- The use of discounted cash flow (DCF) and net present value (NPV) to evaluate investment opportunities causes managers to underestimate the real returns and benefits of proceeding with investments in innovation.

- The way that fixed and sunk costs are considered when evaluating future investments confers an unfair advantage on challengers and shackles incumbent firms that attempt to respond to an attack.

Idea in Brief

Most companies aren't half as innovative as their senior executives want them to be (or as their marketing claims suggest they are). What's stifling innovation? There are plenty of usual suspects, but the authors finger three financial tools as key accomplices. Discounted cash flow and net present value, as commonly used, underestimate the real returns and benefits of proceeding with an investment. Most executives compare the cash flows from innovation against the default scenario of doing nothing, assuming—incorrectly—that the present health of the company will persist indefinitely if the investment is not made. In most situations, however, competitors' sustaining and disruptive investments over time result in deterioration of financial performance. Fixed- and sunk-cost conventional wisdom confers an unfair advantage on challengers and shackles incumbent firms that attempt to respond to an attack.

Executives in established companies, bemoaning the expense of building new brands and developing new sales and distribution channels, seek instead to leverage their existing brands and structures. Entrants, in contrast, simply create new ones. The problem for the incumbent isn't that the challenger can spend more; it's that the challenger is spared the dilemma of having to choose between full-cost and marginal-cost options. The emphasis on short-term earnings per share as the primary driver of share price, and hence shareholder value creation, acts to restrict investments in innovative long-term growth opportunities. These are not bad tools and concepts in and of themselves, but the way they are used to evaluate investments creates a systematic bias against successful innovation. The authors recommend alternative methods that can help managers innovate with a much more astute eye for future value.

- The emphasis on earnings per share as the primary driver of share price and hence of shareholder value creation, to the exclusion of almost everything else, diverts resources away from investments whose payoff lies beyond the immediate horizon.

These are not bad tools and concepts, we hasten to add. But the way they are commonly wielded in evaluating investments creates a systematic bias against innovation. We will recommend alternative methods that, in our experience, can help managers innovate with a much more astute eye for future value. Our primary aim, though,

The DCF trap

Most executives compare the cash flows from innovation against the default scenario of doing nothing, assuming—incorrectly—that the present health of the company will persist indefinitely if the investment is not made. For a better assessment of the innovation's value, the comparison should be between its projected discounted cash flow and the more likely scenario of a decline in performance in the absence of innovation investment.

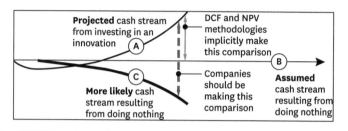

is simply to bring these concerns to light in the hope that others with deeper expertise may be inspired to examine and resolve them.

Misapplying Discounted Cash Flow and Net Present Value

The first of the misleading and misapplied tools of financial analysis is the method of discounting cash flow to calculate the net present value of an initiative. Discounting a future stream of cash flows into a "present value" assumes that a rational investor would be indifferent to having a dollar today or to receiving some years from now a dollar plus the interest or return that could be earned by investing that dollar for those years. With that as an operating principle, it makes perfect sense to assess investments by dividing the money to be received in future years by $(1 + r)^n$, where r is the discount rate—the annual return from investing that money—and n is the number of years during which the investment could be earning that return.

While the mathematics of discounting is logically impeccable, analysts commonly commit two errors that create an anti-innovation bias. The first error is to assume that the base case of not investing in the innovation—the do-nothing scenario against which cash flows from the innovation are compared—is that the present health of the company will persist indefinitely into the future if the investment is not made. As shown in the exhibit "The DCF trap," the mathematics considers the investment in isolation and compares the present value of the innovation's cash stream less project costs with the cash stream in the absence of the investment, which is assumed to be unchanging. In most situations, however, competitors' sustaining and disruptive investments over time result in price and margin pressure, technology changes, market share losses, sales volume decreases, and a declining stock price. As Eileen Rudden at Boston Consulting Group pointed out, the most likely stream of cash for the company in the do-nothing scenario is not a continuation of the status quo. It is a nonlinear decline in performance.

It's tempting but wrong to assess the value of a proposed investment by measuring whether it will make us better off than we are now. It's wrong because, if things are deteriorating on their own, we might be worse off than we are now after we make the proposed investment but better off than we would have been without it. Philip Bobbitt calls this logic Parmenides' Fallacy, after the ancient Greek logician who claimed to have proved that conditions in the real world must necessarily be unchanging. Analysts who attempt to distill the value of an innovation into one simple number that they can compare with other simple numbers are generally trapped by Parmenides' Fallacy.

It's hard to accurately forecast the stream of cash from an investment in innovation. It is even more difficult to forecast the extent to which a firm's financial performance may deteriorate in the absence of the investment. But this analysis must be done. Remember the response that good economists are taught to offer to the question "How are you?" It is "Relative to what?" This is a crucial question. Answering it entails assessing the projected value of the innovation against a range of scenarios, the most realistic of which is often a deteriorating competitive and financial future.

The second set of problems with discounted cash flow calculations relates to errors of estimation. Future cash flows, especially those generated by disruptive investments, are difficult to predict. Numbers for the "out years" can be a complete shot in the dark. To cope with what cannot be known, analysts often project a year-by-year stream of numbers for three to five years and then "punt" by calculating a terminal value to account for everything thereafter. The logic, of course, is that the year-to-year estimates for distant years are so imprecise as to be no more accurate than a terminal value. To calculate a terminal value, analysts divide the cash to be generated in the last year for which they've done a specific estimate by $(r-g)$, the discount rate minus the projected growth rate in cash flows from that time on. They then discount that single number back to the present. In our experience, assumed terminal values often account for more than half of a project's total NPV.

Terminal value numbers, based as they are on estimates for preceding years, tend to amplify errors contained in early-year assumptions. More worrisome still, terminal value doesn't allow for the scenario testing that we described above—contrasting the result of this investment with the deterioration in performance that is the most likely result of doing nothing. And yet, because of market inertia, competitors' development cycles, and the typical pace of disruption, it is often in the fifth year or beyond—the point at which terminal value factors in—that the decline of the enterprise in the do-nothing scenario begins to accelerate.

Arguably, a root cause of companies' persistent underinvestment in the innovations required to sustain long-term success is the indiscriminate and oversimplified use of NPV as an analytical tool. Still, we understand the desire to quantify streams of cash that defy quantification and then to distill those streams into a single number that can be compared with other single numbers: It is an attempt to translate cacophonous articulations of the future into a language—numbers—that everyone can read and compare. We hope to show that numbers are not the only language into which the value of future investments can be translated—and that there are, in fact, other, better languages that all members of a management team can understand.

Using Fixed and Sunk Costs Unwisely

The second widely misapplied paradigm of financial decision making relates to fixed and sunk costs. When evaluating a future course of action, the argument goes, managers should consider only the future or marginal cash outlays (either capital or expense) that are required for an innovation investment, subtract those outlays from the marginal cash that is likely to flow in, and discount the resulting net flow to the present. As with the paradigm of DCF and NPV, there is nothing wrong with the mathematics of this principle—as long as the capabilities required for yesterday's success are adequate for tomorrow's as well. When new capabilities are required for future success, however, this margining on fixed and sunk costs biases managers toward leveraging assets and capabilities that are likely to become obsolete.

For the purposes of this discussion we'll define fixed costs as those whose level is independent of the level of output. Typical fixed costs include general and administrative costs: salaries and benefits, insurance, taxes, and so on. (Variable costs include things like raw materials, commissions, and pay to temporary workers.) Sunk costs are those portions of fixed costs that are irrevocably committed, typically including investments in buildings and capital equipment and R&D costs.

An example from the steel industry illustrates how fixed and sunk costs make it difficult for companies that can and should invest in new capabilities actually to do so. In the late 1960s, steel minimills such as Nucor and Chaparral began disrupting integrated steelmakers such as U.S. Steel (USX), picking off customers in the least-demanding product tiers of each market and then moving relentlessly upmarket, using their 20% cost advantage to capture first the rebar market and then the bar and rod, angle iron, and structural beam markets. By 1988 the minimills had driven the higher-cost integrated mills out of lower-tier products, and Nucor had begun building its first minimill to roll sheet steel in Crawfordsville, Indiana. Nucor estimated that for an investment of $260 million it could sell 800,000 tons of steel annually at a price of $350 per ton. The cash cost to produce a ton of sheet steel in the Crawfordsville mill would be $270. When the timing of cash flows was taken into account, the internal rate of return to Nucor on this investment was over 20%—substantially higher than Nucor's weighted average cost of capital.

Incumbent USX recognized that the minimills constituted a grave threat. Using a new technology called continuous strip production, Nucor had now entered the sheet steel market, albeit with an inferior-quality product, at a significantly lower cost per ton. And Nucor's track record of vigilant improvement meant that the quality of its sheet steel would improve with production experience. Despite this understanding, USX engineers did not even consider building a greenfield minimill like the one Nucor built. The reason? It seemed more profitable to leverage the old technology than to create the new. USX's existing mills, which used traditional technology, had 30% excess capacity, and the marginal cash cost of producing an extra ton of steel by leveraging that excess capacity was less than $50 per ton. When USX's financial analysts contrasted the marginal cash flow of $300 ($350 revenue minus the $50 marginal cost) with the average cash flow of $80 per ton in a greenfield mill, investment in a new low-cost minimill made no sense. What's more, USX's plants were depreciated, so the marginal cash flow of $300 on a low asset base looked very attractive.

And therein lies the rub. Nucor, the attacker, had no fixed or sunk cost investments on which to do a marginal cost calculation. To Nucor, the full cost was the marginal cost. Crawfordsville was the only choice on its menu—and because the IRR was attractive, the decision was simple. USX, in contrast, had two choices on its menu: It could build a greenfield plant like Nucor's with a lower average cost per ton or it could utilize more fully its existing facility.

So what happened? Nucor has continued to improve its process, move upmarket, and gain market share with more efficient continuous strip production capabilities, while USX has relied on the capabilities that had been built to succeed in the past. USX's strategy to maximize marginal profit, in other words, caused the company not to minimize long-term average costs. As a result, the company is locked into an escalating cycle of commitment to a failing strategy.

The attractiveness of any investment can be completely assessed only when it is compared with the attractiveness of the right alternatives on a menu of investments. When a company is looking at adding capacity that is identical to existing capacity, it makes sense to compare the marginal cost of leveraging the old with the full cost of creating the new. But when new technologies or capabilities are required for future competitiveness, margining on the past will send you down the wrong path. The argument that investment decisions should be based on marginal costs is always correct. But when creating new capabilities is the issue, the relevant marginal cost is actually the full cost of creating the new.

When we look at fixed and sunk costs from this perspective, several anomalies we have observed in our studies of innovation are explained. Executives in established companies bemoan how expensive it is to build new brands and develop new sales and distribution channels—so they seek instead to leverage their existing brands and structures. Entrants, in contrast, simply create new ones. The problem for the incumbent isn't that the challenger can outspend it; it's that the challenger is spared the dilemma of having to choose between full-cost and marginal-cost options. We have repeatedly observed leading, established companies misapply fixed-and-sunk-cost doctrine and rely on assets and capabilities that were forged in the past to succeed in the future. In doing so, they fail to make the same investments that entrants and attackers find to be profitable.

A related misused financial practice that biases managers against investment in needed future capabilities is that of using a capital asset's estimated *usable* lifetime as the period over which it should be depreciated. This causes problems when the asset's usable lifetime is longer than its *competitive* lifetime. Managers who depreciate assets according to the more gradual schedule of usable life often face massive write-offs when those assets become competitively obsolete and need to be replaced with newer-technology assets. This was the situation confronting the integrated steelmakers. When building new capabilities entails writing off the old, incumbents face a hit to quarterly earnings that disruptive entrants to the industry do not.

Knowing that the equity markets will punish them for a write-off, managers may stall in adopting new technology.

This may be part of the reason for the dramatic increase in private equity buyouts over the past decade and the recent surge of interest in technology-oriented industries. As disruptions continue to shorten the competitive lifetime of major investments made only three to five years ago, more companies find themselves needing to take asset write-downs or to significantly restructure their business models. These are wrenching changes that are often made more easily and comfortably outside the glare of the public markets.

What's the solution to this dilemma? Michael Mauboussin at Legg Mason Capital Management suggests it is to value *strategies,* not projects. When an attacker is gaining ground, executives at the incumbent companies need to do their investment analyses in the same way the attackers do—by focusing on the strategies that will ensure long-term competitiveness. This is the only way they can see the world as the attackers see it and the only way they can predict the consequences of not investing.

No manager would consciously decide to destroy a company by leveraging the competencies of the past while ignoring those required for the future. Yet this is precisely what many of them do. They do it because strategy and finance were taught as separate topics in business school. Their professors of financial modeling alluded to the importance of strategy, and their strategy professors occasionally referred to value creation, but little time was spent on a thoughtful integration of the two. This bifurcation persists in most companies, where responsibilities for strategy and finance reside in the realms of different vice presidents. Because a firm's actual strategy is defined by the stream of projects in which it does or doesn't invest, finance and strategy need to be studied and practiced in an integrated way.

Focusing Myopically on Earnings per Share

A third financial paradigm that leads established companies to underinvest in innovation is the emphasis on earnings per share as the primary driver of share price and hence of shareholder value creation. Managers are under so much pressure, from various directions, to focus on short-term stock performance that they pay less attention to the company's long-term health than they might—to the point where they're reluctant to invest in innovations that don't pay off immediately.

Where's the pressure coming from? To answer that question, we need to look briefly at the principal-agent theory—the doctrine that the interests of shareholders (principals) aren't aligned with those of managers (agents). Without powerful financial incentives to focus the interests of principals and agents on maximizing shareholder value, the thinking goes, agents will pursue other agendas—and in the process, may neglect to pay enough attention to efficiencies or squander capital investments on pet projects—at the expense of profits that ought to accrue to the principals.

That conflict of incentives has been taught so aggressively that the compensation of most senior executives in publicly traded companies is now heavily weighted away from salaries and toward packages that reward improvements in share price. That in turn has led to an almost singular focus on earnings per share and EPS growth as *the* metric for corporate performance. While we all recognize the importance of other indicators such as market position, brands, intellectual capital, and long-term competitiveness, the bias is toward using a simple quantitative indicator that is easily compared period to period and across companies. And because EPS growth is an important driver of near-term share price improvement, managers are biased against investments that will compromise near-term EPS. Many decide instead to use the excess cash on the balance sheet to buy back the company's stock under the guise of "returning money to shareholders." But although contracting the number of shares pumps up earnings per share, sometimes quite dramatically, it does nothing to enhance the underlying value of the enterprise and may even damage it by restricting the flow of cash available for investment in potentially disruptive products and business models. Indeed, some have fingered share-price-based incentive compensation packages as a key driver of the share price manipulation that captured so many business headlines in the early 2000s.

The myopic focus on EPS is not just about the money. CEOs and corporate managers who are more concerned with their reputations than with amassing more wealth also focus on stock price and short-term performance measures such as quarterly earnings. They know that, to a large extent, others' perception of their success is tied up in those numbers, leading to a self-reinforcing cycle of obsession. This behavior cycle is amplified when there is an "earnings surprise." Equity prices over the short term respond positively to upside earnings surprises (and negatively to downside surprises), so investors have no incentive to look at rational measures of long-term performance. To the contrary, they are rewarded for going with the market's short-term model.

The active leveraged buyout market has further reinforced the focus on EPS. Companies that are viewed as having failed to maximize value, as evidenced by a lagging share price, are vulnerable to overtures from outsiders, including corporate raiders or hedge funds that seek to increase their near-term stock price by putting a company into play or by replacing the CEO. Thus, while the past two decades have witnessed a dramatic increase in the proportion of CEO compensation tied to stock price—and a breathtaking increase in CEO compensation overall—they have witnessed a concomitant decrease in the average tenure of CEOs. Whether you believe that CEOs are most motivated by the carrot (major increases in compensation and wealth) or the stick (the threat of the company being sold or of being replaced), you should not be surprised to find so many CEOs focused on current earnings per share as the best predictor of stock price, sometimes to the exclusion of anything else. One study even showed that senior executives were routinely willing to sacrifice long-term shareholder value to meet earnings expectations or to smooth reported earnings.

We suspect that the principal-agent theory is misapplied. Most traditional principals—by which we mean shareholders—don't themselves have incentives to watch out for the long-term health of a company. Over 90% of the shares of publicly traded companies in the United States are held in the portfolios of mutual funds, pension funds, and hedge funds. The average holding period for stocks in these portfolios is less than 10 months—leading us to prefer the term "share owner" as a more accurate description than "shareholder." As for agents, we believe that most executives work tirelessly, throwing their hearts and minds into their jobs, not because they are paid an incentive to do so but because they love what they do. Tying executive compensation to stock prices, therefore, does not affect the intensity or energy or intelligence with which executives perform. But it does direct their efforts toward activities whose impact can be felt within the holding horizon of the typical share owner and within the measurement horizon of the incentive—both of which are less than one year.

Ironically, most so-called principals today are themselves agents—agents of other people's mutual funds, investment portfolios, endowments, and retirement programs. For these agents, the enterprise in which they are investing has no inherent interest or value beyond providing a platform for improving the short-term financial metric by which their fund's performance is measured and their own compensation is determined. And, in a final grand but sad irony, the real principals (the people who put their money into mutual funds and pension plans, sometimes through yet another layer of agents) are frequently the very individuals whose long-term employment is jeopardized when the focus on short-term EPS acts to restrict investments in innovative growth opportunities. We suggest that the principal-agent theory is obsolete in this context. What we really have is an *agent-agent* problem, where the desires and goals of the agent for the share owners compete with the desires and goals of the agents running the company. The incentives are still misaligned, but managers should not capitulate on the basis of an obsolete paradigm.

Processes That Support (or Sabotage) Innovation

As we have seen, managers in established corporations use analytical methods that make innovation investments extremely difficult to justify. As it happens, the most common system for green-lighting investment projects only reinforces the flaws inherent in the tools and dogmas discussed earlier.

Stage-gate innovation

Most established companies start by considering a broad range of possible innovations; they winnow out the less viable ideas, step by step, until only the most promising ones remain. Most such processes include three stages: feasibility, development, and launch. The stages are separated by stage gates: review meetings at which project teams report to senior managers what they've accomplished. On the basis of this progress and the project's potential, the gatekeepers approve the passage of the initiative into the next phase, return it to the previous stage for more work, or kill it.

Many marketers and engineers regard the stage-gate development process with disdain. Why? Because the key decision criteria at each gate are the size of projected revenues and profits from the product and the associated risks. Revenues from products that incrementally improve upon those the company is currently selling can be credibly quantified. But proposals to create growth by exploiting potentially disruptive technologies, products, or business models can't be bolstered by hard numbers. Their markets are initially small, and substantial revenues generally don't materialize for several years. When these projects are pitted against incremental sustaining innovations in the battle for funding, the incremental ones sail through while the seemingly riskier ones get delayed or die.

The process itself has two serious drawbacks. First, project teams generally know how good the projections (such as NPV) need to look in order to win funding, and it takes only nanoseconds to tweak an assumption and run another full scenario to get a faltering project over the hurdle rate. If, as is often the case, there are eight to 10 assumptions underpinning the financial model, changing only a few of them by a mere 2% or 3% each may do the trick. It is then difficult for the senior managers who sit as gatekeepers to even discern which are the salient assumptions, let alone judge whether they are realistic.

The second drawback is that the stage-gate system assumes that the proposed strategy is the right strategy. Once an innovation has been approved, developed, and launched, all that remains is skillful execution. If, after launch, a product falls seriously short of the projections (and 75% of them do), it is canceled. The problem is that, except in the case of incremental innovations, the right strategy—especially which job the customer wants done—cannot be completely known in advance. It must emerge and then be refined.

The stage-gate system is not suited to the task of assessing innovations whose purpose is to build new growth businesses, but most companies continue to follow it simply because they see no alternative.

Discovery-driven planning

Happily, though, there are alternative systems specifically designed to support intelligent investments in future growth. One such process, which Rita Gunther McGrath and Ian MacMillan call *discovery-driven planning,* has the potential to greatly improve the success rate. Discovery-driven planning essentially reverses the sequence of some of the steps in the stage-gate process. Its logic is elegantly simple. If the project teams all know how good the numbers need to look in order to win funding, why go through the charade of making and revising assumptions in order to fabricate an acceptable set of numbers? Why not just put the minimally acceptable revenue, income, and cash flow statement as the standard first page of the gate documents? The second page can then raise the critical issues: "Okay. So we all know this is how good the numbers need to look. What set of assumptions must prove true in order for these numbers to materialize?" The project team creates from that analysis an assumptions checklist—a list of things that need to prove true for the project to succeed. The items on the checklist are rank-ordered, with the deal killers and the assumptions that can be tested with little expense toward the top. McGrath and MacMillan call this a "reverse income statement."

When a project enters a new stage, the assumptions checklist is used as the basis of the project plan for that stage. This is not a plan to execute, however. It is a plan to *learn*—to test as quickly and at as low a cost as possible whether the assumptions upon which success is predicated are actually valid. If a critical assumption proves not to be valid, the project team must revise its strategy until the assumptions upon which it is built are all plausible. If no set of plausible assumptions will support the case for success, the project is killed.

Traditional stage-gate planning obfuscates the assumptions and shines the light on the financial projections. But there is no need to focus the analytical spotlight on the numbers, because the desirability of attractive numbers has never been the question. Discovery-driven planning shines a spotlight on the place where senior management needs illumination—the assumptions that constitute the key uncertainties. More often than not, failure in innovation is rooted in not having asked an important question, rather than in having arrived at an incorrect answer.

Today, processes like discovery-driven planning are more commonly used in entrepreneurial settings than in the large corporations that desperately need them. We hope that by recounting the strengths of one such system we'll persuade established corporations to reassess how they make decisions about investment projects.

We keep rediscovering that the root reason for established companies' failure to innovate is that managers don't have good tools to help them understand markets, build brands, find customers, select employees, organize teams, and develop strategy. Some of the tools typically used for financial analysis, and decision making about investments, distort the value, importance, and likelihood of success of investments in innovation. There's a better way for management teams to grow their companies. But they will need the courage to challenge some of the paradigms of financial analysis and the willingness to develop alternative methodologies.

Originally published in January 2008. Reprint R0801F

Reinventing Your Business Model

by Mark W. Johnson, Clayton M. Christensen, and Henning Kagermann

IN 2003, APPLE INTRODUCED the iPod with the iTunes store, revolutionizing portable entertainment, creating a new market, and transforming the company. In just three years, the iPod/iTunes combination became a nearly $10 billion product, accounting for almost 50% of Apple's revenue. Apple's market capitalization catapulted from around $1 billion in early 2003 to over $150 billion by late 2007.

This success story is well known; what's less well known is that Apple was not the first to bring digital music players to market. A company called Diamond Multimedia introduced the Rio in 1998. Another firm, Best Data, introduced the Cabo 64 in 2000. Both products worked well and were portable and stylish. So why did the iPod, rather than the Rio or Cabo, succeed?

Apple did something far smarter than take a good technology and wrap it in a snazzy design. It took a good technology and wrapped it in a great business model. Apple's true innovation was to make downloading digital music easy and convenient. To do that, the company built a groundbreaking business model that combined hardware, software, and service. This approach worked like Gillette's famous blades-and-razor model in reverse: Apple essentially gave away the "blades" (low-margin iTunes music) to lock in purchase of the "razor" (the high-margin iPod). That model defined value in a new way and provided game-changing convenience to the consumer.

Business model innovations have reshaped entire industries and redistributed billions of dollars of value. Retail discounters such as Wal-Mart and Target, which entered the market with pioneering business models, now account for 75% of the total valuation of the retail sector. Low-cost U.S. airlines grew from a blip on the radar screen to 55% of the market value of all carriers. Fully 11 of the 27 companies born in the last quarter century that grew their way into the *Fortune* 500 in the past 10 years did so through business model innovation.

Stories of business model innovation from well-established companies like Apple, however, are rare. An analysis of major innovations within existing corporations in the past decade shows that precious few have been business-model related. And a recent American Management Association study determined that no more than 10% of innovation investment at global companies is focused on developing new business models.

Yet everyone's talking about it. A 2005 survey by the Economist Intelligence Unit reported that over 50% of executives believe business model innovation will become even more important for success than product or service innovation. A 2008 IBM survey of corporate CEOs echoed these results. Nearly all of the CEOs polled reported the need to adapt their business models; more than two-thirds said that extensive changes were required. And in these tough economic times, some CEOs are already looking to business model innovation to address permanent shifts in their market landscapes.

Senior managers at incumbent companies thus confront a frustrating question: Why is it so difficult to pull off the new growth that business model innovation can bring? Our research suggests two problems. The first is a lack of definition: Very little formal study has been done into the dynamics and processes of business model development. Second, few companies understand their existing business model well enough—the premise behind its development, its natural interdependencies, and its strengths and limitations. So they don't know when they can leverage their core business and when success requires a new business model.

Idea in Brief

When Apple introduced the iPod, it did something far smarter than wrap a good technology in a snazzy design. It wrapped a good technology in a **great business model**. Combining hardware, software, and service, the model provided game-changing convenience for consumers *and* record-breaking profits for Apple.

Great business models can reshape industries and drive spectacular growth. Yet many companies find business-model innovation difficult. Managers don't understand their existing model well enough to know when it needs changing—or how.

To determine whether your firm should alter its business model, Johnson, Christensen, and Kagermann advise these steps:

1. Articulate what makes your existing model successful. For example, what customer problem does it solve? How does it make money for your firm?

2. Watch for signals that your model needs changing, such as tough new competitors on the horizon.

3. Decide whether reinventing your model is worth the effort. The answer's yes only if the new model changes the industry or market.

After tackling these problems with dozens of companies, we have found that new business models often look unattractive to internal and external stakeholders—at the outset. To see past the borders of what is and into the land of the new, companies need a road map.

Ours consists of three simple steps. The first is to realize that success starts by not thinking about business models at all. It starts with thinking about the opportunity to satisfy a real customer who needs a job done. The second step is to construct a blueprint laying out how your company will fulfill that need at a profit. In our model, that plan has four elements. The third is to compare that model to your existing model to see how much you'd have to change it to capture the opportunity. Once you do, you will know if you can use your existing model and organization or need to separate out a new unit to execute a new model. Every successful company is already fulfilling a real customer need with an effective business model, whether that model is explicitly understood or not. Let's take a look at what that entails.

Idea in Practice

Understand Your Current Business Model

A successful model has these components:

- **Customer value proposition.** The model helps customers perform a specific "job" that alternative offerings don't address.

  Example: MinuteClinics enable people to visit a doctor's office without appointments by making nurse practitioners available to treat minor health issues.

- **Profit formula.** The model generates value for your company through factors such as revenue model, cost structure, margins, and inventory turnover.

  Example: The Tata Group's inexpensive car, the Nano, is profitable because the company has reduced many cost structure elements, accepted lower-than-standard gross margins, and sold the Nano in large volumes to its target market: first-time car buyers in emerging markets.

- **Key resources and processes.** Your company has the people, technology, products, facilities, equipment, and brand required to deliver the value proposition to your targeted customers. And it has processes (training, manufacturing, service) to leverage those resources.

  Example: For Tata Motors to fulfill the requirements of the Nano's profit formula, it had to reconceive how a car is designed, manufactured, and distributed. It redefined its supplier strategy, choosing to outsource a remarkable 85% of the Nano's components and to use nearly 60% fewer vendors than normal to reduce transaction costs.

Identify When a New Model May Be Needed

These circumstances often require business model change:

Business Model: A Definition

A business model, from our point of view, consists of four interlocking elements that, taken together, create and deliver value. The most important to get right, by far, is the first.

Customer value proposition (CVP)

A successful company is one that has found a way to create value for customers—that is, a way to help customers get an important job

An *opportunity* to . . .	Example
Address needs of large groups who find existing solutions too expensive or complicated.	The Nano's goal is to open car ownership to low-income consumers in emerging markets.
Capitalize on new technology, or leverage existing technologies in new markets.	A company develops a commercial application for a technology originally developed for military use.
Bring a job-to-be-done focus where it doesn't exist.	FedEx focused on performing customers' unmet "job": Receive packages faster and more reliably than any other service could.

A *need* to . . .	Example
Fend off low-end disruptors.	Mini-mills threatened the integrated steel mills a generation ago by making steel at significantly lower prices.
Respond to shifts in competition.	Power-tool maker Hilti switched from selling to renting its tools in part because "good enough" low-end entrants had begun chipping away at the market for selling high-quality tools.

done. By "job" we mean a fundamental problem in a given situation that needs a solution. Once we understand the job and all its dimensions, including the full process for how to get it done, we can design the offering. The more important the job is to the customer, the lower the level of customer satisfaction with current options for getting the job done, and the better your solution is than existing alternatives at getting the job done (and, of course, the lower the price), the greater the CVP. Opportunities for creating a CVP are at their most potent, we have found, when alternative products and services have not been designed with the real job in mind and you can design an offering that gets that job—and only that job—done perfectly. We'll come back to that point later.

Profit formula

The profit formula is the blueprint that defines how the company creates value for itself while providing value to the customer. It consists of the following:

- *Revenue model:* price x volume

- *Cost structure:* direct costs, indirect costs, economies of scale. Cost structure will be predominantly driven by the cost of the key resources required by the business model.

- *Margin model:* given the expected volume and cost structure, the contribution needed from each transaction to achieve desired profits.

- *Resource velocity:* how fast we need to turn over inventory, fixed assets, and other assets—and, overall, how well we need to utilize resources—to support our expected volume and achieve our anticipated profits.

People often think the terms "profit formulas" and "business models" are interchangeable. But how you make a profit is only one piece of the model. We've found it most useful to start by setting the price required to deliver the CVP and then work backwards from there to determine what the variable costs and gross margins must be. This then determines what the scale and resource velocity needs to be to achieve the desired profits.

Key resources

The key resources are assets such as the people, technology, products, facilities, equipment, channels, and brand required to deliver the value proposition to the targeted customer. The focus here is on the *key* elements that create value for the customer and the company, and the way those elements interact. (Every company also has generic resources that do not create competitive differentiation.)

Key processes
Successful companies have operational and managerial processes that allow them to deliver value in a way they can successfully repeat and increase in scale. These may include such recurrent tasks as training, development, manufacturing, budgeting, planning, sales, and service. Key processes also include a company's rules, metrics, and norms.

These four elements form the building blocks of any business. The customer value proposition and the profit formula define value for the customer and the company, respectively; key resources and key processes describe how that value will be delivered to both the customer and the company.

As simple as this framework may seem, its power lies in the complex interdependencies of its parts. Major changes to any of these four elements affect the others and the whole. Successful businesses devise a more or less stable system in which these elements bond to one another in consistent and complementary ways.

How Great Models Are Built

To illustrate the elements of our business model framework, we will look at what's behind two companies' game-changing business model innovations.

Creating a customer value proposition
It's not possible to invent or reinvent a business model without first identifying a clear customer value proposition. Often, it starts as a quite simple realization. Imagine, for a moment, that you are standing on a Mumbai road on a rainy day. You notice the large number of motor scooters snaking precariously in and out around the cars. As you look more closely, you see that most bear whole families—both parents and several children. Your first thought might be "That's

The Elements of a Successful Business Model

EVERY SUCCESSFUL COMPANY ALREADY operates according to an effective business model. By systematically identifying all of its constituent parts, executives can understand how the model fulfills a potent value proposition in a profitable way using certain key resources and key processes. With that understanding, they can then judge how well the same model could be used to fulfill a radically different CVP—and what they'd need to do to construct a new one, if need be, to capitalize on that opportunity.

Customer Value Proposition (CVP)
- **Target customer**
- **Job to be done** to solve an important problem or fulfill an important need for the target customer
- **Offering**, which satisfies the problem or fulfills the need. This is defined not only by what is sold but also by how it's sold.

PROFIT FORMULA
- **Revenue model** How much money can be made: price x volume. Volume can be thought of in terms of market size, purchase frequency, ancillary sales, etc.

- **Cost structure** How costs are allocated: includes cost of key assets, direct costs, indirect costs, economies of scale.

- **Margin model** How much each transaction should net to achieve desired profit levels.

- **Resource velocity** How quickly resources need to be used to support target volume. Includes lead times, throughput, inventory turns, asset utilization, and so on.

KEY RESOURCES
needed to deliver the customer value proposition profitably. Might include:
- **People**
- **Technology, products**
- **Equipment**
- **Information**
- **Channels**
- **Partnerships, alliances**
- **Brand**

KEY PROCESSES, as well as rules, metrics, and norms, that make the profitable delivery of the customer value proposition repeatable and scalable. Might include:
- **Processes:** design, product development, sourcing, manufacturing, marketing, hiring and training, IT

- **Rules and metrics:** margin requirements for investment, credit terms, lead times, supplier terms

- **Norms:** opportunity size needed for investment, approach to customers and channels

crazy!" or "That's the way it is in developing countries—people get by as best they can."

When Ratan Tata of Tata Group looked out over this scene, he saw a critical job to be done: providing a safer alternative for scooter families. He understood that the cheapest car available in India cost easily five times what a scooter did and that many of these families could not afford one. Offering an affordable, safer, all-weather alternative for scooter families was a powerful value proposition, one with the potential to reach tens of millions of people who were not yet part of the car-buying market. Ratan Tata also recognized that Tata Motors' business model could not be used to develop such a product at the needed price point.

At the other end of the market spectrum, Hilti, a Liechtenstein-based manufacturer of high-end power tools for the construction industry, reconsidered the real job to be done for many of its current customers. A contractor makes money by finishing projects; if the required tools aren't available and functioning properly, the job doesn't get done. Contractors don't make money by *owning* tools; they make it by using them as efficiently as possible. Hilti could help contractors get the job done by selling tool *use* instead of the tools themselves—managing its customers' tool inventory by providing the best tool at the right time and quickly furnishing tool repairs, replacements, and upgrades, all for a monthly fee. To deliver on that value proposition, the company needed to create a fleet-management program for tools and in the process shift its focus from manufacturing and distribution to service. That meant Hilti had to construct a new profit formula and develop new resources and new processes.

The most important attribute of a customer value proposition is its precision: how perfectly it nails the customer job to be done—and nothing else. But such precision is often the most difficult thing to achieve. Companies trying to create the new often neglect to focus on *one* job; they dilute their efforts by attempting to do lots of things. In doing lots of things, they do nothing *really* well.

One way to generate a precise customer value proposition is to think about the four most common barriers keeping people from

Hilti Sidesteps Commoditization

HILTI IS CAPITALIZING ON a game-changing opportunity to increase profitability by turning products into a service. Rather than sell tools (at lower and lower prices), it's selling a "just-the-tool-you-need-when-you-need-it, no-repair-or-storage-hassles" service. Such a radical change in customer value proposition required a shift in all parts of its business model.

Traditional power tool company		Hilti's tool fleet management service
Sales of industrial and professional power tools and accessories	**Customer value proposition**	Leasing a comprehensive fleet of tools to increase contractors's on-site productivity
Low margins, high inventory turnover	**Profit formula**	Higher margins; asset heavy; monthly payments for tool maintenance, repair, and replacement
Distribution channel, low-cost manufacturing plants in developing countries, R&D	**Key resources and processes**	Strong direct-sales approach, contract management, IT systems for inventory management and repair, warehousing

getting particular jobs done: insufficient wealth, access, skill, or time. Software maker Intuit devised QuickBooks to fulfill small-business owners' need to avoid running out of cash. By fulfilling that job with greatly simplified accounting software, Intuit broke the *skills barrier* that kept untrained small-business owners from using more-complicated accounting packages. MinuteClinic, the drugstore-based basic health care provider, broke the *time barrier* that kept people from visiting a doctor's office with minor health issues by making nurse practitioners available without appointments.

Designing a profit formula
Ratan Tata knew the only way to get families off their scooters and into cars would be to break the *wealth barrier* by drastically decreasing the

price of the car. "What if I can change the game and make a car for one lakh?" Tata wondered, envisioning a price point of around US$2,500, less than half the price of the cheapest car available. This, of course, had dramatic ramifications for the profit formula: It required both a significant drop in gross margins and a radical reduction in many elements of the cost structure. He knew, however, he could still make money if he could increase sales volume dramatically, and he knew that his target base of consumers was potentially huge.

For Hilti, moving to a contract management program required shifting assets from customers' balance sheets to its own and generating revenue through a lease/subscription model. For a monthly fee, customers could have a full complement of tools at their fingertips, with repair and maintenance included. This would require a fundamental shift in all major components of the profit formula: the revenue stream (pricing, the staging of payments, and how to think about volume), the cost structure (including added sales development and contract management costs), and the supporting margins and transaction velocity.

Identifying key resources and processes

Having articulated the value proposition for both the customer and the business, companies must then consider the key resources and processes needed to deliver that value. For a professional services firm, for example, the key resources are generally its people, and the key processes are naturally people related (training and development, for instance). For a packaged goods company, strong brands and well-selected channel retailers might be the key resources, and associated brand-building and channel-management processes among the critical processes.

Oftentimes, it's not the individual resources and processes that make the difference but their relationship to one another. Companies will almost always need to integrate their key resources and processes in a unique way to get a job done perfectly for a set of customers. When they do, they almost always create enduring competitive advantage. Focusing first on the value proposition and the profit formula makes clear how those resources and processes need to interrelate. For example, most general hospitals offer a value proposition that might be described as, "We'll do anything for anybody." Being all things to all people requires these hospitals to have a vast collection of resources (specialists, equipment, and so on) that can't be knit together in any proprietary way. The result is not just a lack of differentiation but dissatisfaction.

By contrast, a hospital that focuses on a specific value proposition can integrate its resources and processes in a unique way that delights customers. National Jewish Health in Denver, for example, is organized around a focused value proposition we'd characterize as, "If you have a disease of the pulmonary system, bring it here. We'll define its root cause and prescribe an effective therapy." Narrowing its focus has allowed National Jewish to develop processes that integrate the ways in which its specialists and specialized equipment work together.

For Tata Motors to fulfill the requirements of its customer value proposition and profit formula for the Nano, it had to reconceive how a car is designed, manufactured, and distributed. Tata built a small team of fairly young engineers who would not, like the company's more-experienced designers, be influenced and constrained in their thinking by the automaker's existing profit formulas. This team dramatically minimized the number of parts in the vehicle, resulting in a significant cost saving. Tata also reconceived its supplier strategy, choosing to outsource a remarkable 85% of the Nano's components and use nearly 60% fewer vendors than normal to reduce transaction costs and achieve better economies of scale.

At the other end of the manufacturing line, Tata is envisioning an entirely new way of assembling and distributing its cars. The ultimate plan is to ship the modular components of the vehicles to a combined network of company-owned and independent entrepreneur-owned assembly plants, which will build them to order. The Nano will be designed, built, distributed, and serviced in a radically new way—one that could not be accomplished without a new business model. And while the jury is still out, Ratan Tata may solve a traffic safety problem in the process.

For Hilti, the greatest challenge lay in training its sales representatives to do a thoroughly new task. Fleet management is not a half-hour sale; it takes days, weeks, even months of meetings to per-suade customers to buy a program instead of a product. Suddenly, field reps accustomed to dealing with crew leaders and on-site pur-chasing managers in mobile trailers found themselves staring down CEOs and CFOs across conference tables.

Additionally, leasing required new resources—new people, more robust IT systems, and other new technologies—to design and de-velop the appropriate packages and then come to an agreement on monthly payments. Hilti needed a process for maintaining large ar-senals of tools more inexpensively and effectively than its customers had. This required warehousing, an inventory management system, and a supply of replacement tools. On the customer management side, Hilti developed a website that enabled construction managers to view all the tools in their fleet and their usage rates. With that information readily available, the managers could easily handle the cost accounting associated with those assets.

Rules, norms, and metrics are often the last element to emerge in a developing business model. They may not be fully envisioned until the new product or service has been road tested. Nor should they be. Business models need to have the flexibility to change in their early years.

When a New Business Model Is Needed

Established companies should not undertake business-model inno-vation lightly. They can often create new products that disrupt com-petitors without fundamentally changing their own business model. Procter & Gamble, for example, developed a number of what it calls "disruptive market innovations" with such products as the Swiffer disposable mop and duster and Febreze, a new kind of air freshener. Both innovations built on P&G's existing business model and its es-tablished dominance in household consumables.

There are clearly times, however, when creating new growth re-quires venturing not only into unknown market territory but also into unknown business model territory. When? The short answer is "When significant changes are needed to all four elements of your existing model." But it's not always that simple. Management judgment is clearly required. That said, we have observed five strategic circumstances that often require business model change:

1. The opportunity to address through disruptive innovation the needs of large groups of potential customers who are shut out of a market entirely because existing solutions are too expensive or complicated for them. This includes the opportunity to democratize products in emerging markets (or reach the bottom of the pyramid), as Tata's Nano does.

2. The opportunity to capitalize on a brand-new technology by wrapping a new business model around it (Apple and MP3 players) or the opportunity to leverage a tested technology by bringing it to a whole new market (say, by offering military technologies in the commercial space or vice versa).

3. The opportunity to bring a job-to-be-done focus where one does not yet exist. That's common in industries where companies focus on products or customer segments, which leads them to refine existing products more and more, increasing commoditization over time. A jobs focus allows companies to redefine industry profitability. For example, when FedEx entered the package delivery market, it did not try to compete through lower prices or better marketing. Instead, it concentrated on fulfilling an entirely unmet customer need to receive packages far, far faster, and more reliably, than any service then could. To do so, it had to integrate its key processes and resources in a vastly more efficient way. The business model that resulted from this job-to-be-done emphasis gave FedEx a significant competitive advantage that took UPS many years to copy.

4. The need to fend off low-end disrupters. If the Nano is successful, it will threaten other automobile makers, much as minimills threatened the integrated steel mills a generation ago by making steel at significantly lower cost.

5. The need to respond to a shifting basis of competition. Inevitably, what defines an acceptable solution in a market will change over time, leading core market segments to commoditize. Hilti needed to change its business model in part because of lower global manufacturing costs; "good enough" low-end entrants had begun chipping away at the market for high-quality power tools.

Of course, companies should not pursue business model reinvention unless they are confident that the opportunity is large enough to warrant the effort. And, there's really no point in instituting a new business model unless it's not only new to the company but in some way new or game-changing to the industry or market. To do otherwise would be a waste of time and money.

These questions will help you evaluate whether the challenge of business model innovation will yield acceptable results. Answering "yes" to all four greatly increases the odds of successful execution:

- Can you nail the job with a focused, compelling customer value proposition?

- Can you devise a model in which all the elements—the customer value proposition, the profit formula, the key resources, and the key processes—work together to get the job done in the most efficient way possible?

- Can you create a new business development process unfettered by the often negative influences of your core business?

- Will the new business model disrupt competitors?

Creating a new model for a new business does not mean the current model is threatened or should be changed. A new model often reinforces and complements the core business, as Dow Corning discovered.

Dow Corning Embraces the Low End

TRADITIONALLY HIGH-MARGIN DOW CORNING found new opportunities in low-margin offerings by setting up a separate business unit that operates in an entirely different way. By fundamentally differentiating its low-end and high-end offerings, the company avoided cannibalizing its traditional business even as it found new profits at the low end.

Established business		New business unit
Customized solutions, negotiated contracts	**Customer value proposition**	No frills, bulk prices, sold through the internet
High-margin, high-overhead retail prices pay for value-added services	**Profit formula**	Spot-market pricing, low overhead to accommodate lower margins, high throughput
R&D, sales, and services orientation	**Key resources and processes**	IT system, lowest-cost processes, maximum automation

How Dow Corning Got Out of Its Own Way

When business model innovation is clearly called for, success lies not only in getting the model right but also in making sure the incumbent business doesn't in some way prevent the new model from creating value or thriving. That was a problem for Dow Corning when it built a new business unit—with a new profit formula—from scratch.

For many years, Dow Corning had sold thousands of silicone-based products and provided sophisticated technical services to an array of industries. After years of profitable growth, however, a number of product areas were stagnating. A strategic review uncovered a critical insight: Its low-end product segment was commoditizing. Many customers experienced in silicone application no longer needed technical services; they needed basic products at low prices. This shift created an opportunity for growth, but to exploit that opportunity Dow Corning had to figure out a way to serve these customers with a lower-priced product. The problem was that both

When the Old Model Will Work

YOU DON'T ALWAYS NEED a new business model to capitalize on a game-changing opportunity. Sometimes, as P&G did with its Swiffer, a company finds that its current model is revolutionary in a new market. When will the old model do? When you can fulfill the new customer value proposition:

- With your current profit formula

- Using most, if not all, of your current key resources and processes

- Using the same core metrics, rules, and norms you now use to run your business

the business model and the culture were built on high-priced, innovative product and service packages. In 2002, in pursuit of what was essentially a commodity business for low-end customers, Dow Corning CEO Gary Anderson asked executive Don Sheets to form a team to start a new business.

The team began by formulating a customer value proposition that it believed would fulfill the job to be done for these price-driven customers. It determined that the price point had to drop 15% (which for a commoditizing material was a huge reduction). As the team analyzed what that new customer value proposition would require, it realized reaching that point was going to take a lot more than merely eliminating services. Dramatic price reduction would call for a different profit formula with a fundamentally lower cost structure, which depended heavily on developing a new IT system. To sell more products faster, the company would need to use the internet to automate processes and reduce overhead as much as possible.

Breaking the rules

As a mature and successful company, Dow Corning was full of highly trained employees used to delivering its high-touch, customized value proposition. To automate, the new business would have to be far more standardized, which meant instituting different and, overall, much stricter rules. For example, order sizes would be limited to a few, larger-volume options; order lead times would fall between two and four weeks (exceptions would cost extra); and credit terms would be fixed. There would be charges if a purchaser required customer service. The writing was on the wall: The new venture would be low-touch, self-service, and standardized. To succeed, Dow Corning would have to break the rules that had previously guided its success.

Sheets next had to determine whether this new venture, with its new rules, could succeed within the confines of Dow Corning's core enterprise. He set up an experimental war game to test how existing staff and systems would react to the requirements of the new customer value proposition. He got crushed as entrenched habits and existing processes thwarted any attempt to change the game. It became clear that the corporate antibodies would kill the initiative before it got off the ground. The way forward was clear: The new venture had to be free from existing rules and free to decide what rules would be appropriate in order for the new commodity line of business to thrive. To nurture the opportunity—and also protect the existing model—a new business unit with a new brand identity was needed. Xiameter was born.

Identifying new competencies

Following the articulation of the new customer value proposition and new profit formula, the Xiameter team focused on the new competencies it would need, its key resources and processes. Information technology, just a small part of Dow Corning's core competencies at that time, emerged as an essential part of the now web-enabled business. Xiameter also needed employees who could make smart decisions very quickly and who would thrive in a fast-changing environment, filled initially with lots of ambiguity. Clearly, new abilities would have to be brought into the business.

Although Xiameter would be established and run as a separate business unit, Don Sheets and the Xiameter team did not want to give up the incumbency advantage that deep knowledge of the industry and of their own products gave them. The challenge was to tap into the expertise without importing the old-rules mind-set.

What Rules, Norms, and Metrics Are Standing in Your Way?

IN ANY BUSINESS, a fundamental understanding of the core model often fades into the mists of institutional memory, but it lives on in rules, norms, and metrics put in place to protect the status quo (for example, "Gross margins must be at 40%"). They are the first line of defense against any new model's taking root in an existing enterprise.

Financial

- Gross margins
- Opportunity size
- Unit pricing
- Unit margin
- Time to breakeven
- Net present value calculations
- Fixed cost investment
- Credit items

Operational

- End-product quality
- Supplier quality
- Owned versus outsourced manufacturing
- Customer service
- Channels
- Lead times
- Throughput

Other

- Pricing
- Performance demands
- Product-development life cycles
- Basis for individuals' rewards and incentives
- Brand parameters

Sheets conducted a focused HR search within Dow Corning for risk takers. During the interview process, when he came across candidates with the right skills, he asked them to take the job on the spot, before they left the room. This approach allowed him to cherry-pick those who could make snap decisions and take big risks.

The secret sauce: patience

Successful new businesses typically revise their business models four times or so on the road to profitability. While a well-considered business-model-innovation process can often shorten this cycle, successful incumbents must tolerate initial failure and grasp the need for course correction. In effect, companies have to focus on learning and adjusting as much as on executing. We recommend companies with new business models be patient for growth (to allow the market opportunity to unfold) but impatient for profit (as an early validation that the model works). A profitable business is the best early indication of a viable model.

Accordingly, to allow for the trial and error that naturally accompanies the creation of the new while also constructing a development cycle that would produce results and demonstrate feasibility with minimal resource outlay, Dow Corning kept the scale of Xiameter's operation small but developed an aggressive timetable for launch and set the goal of becoming profitable by the end of year one.

Xiameter paid back Dow Corning's investment in just three months and went on to become a major, transformative success. Beforehand, Dow Corning had had no online sales component; now 30% of sales originate online, nearly three times the industry average. Most of these customers are new to the company. Far from cannibalizing existing customers, Xiameter has actually supported the main business, allowing Dow Corning's salespeople to more easily enforce premium pricing for their core offerings while providing a viable alternative for the price-conscious.

Established companies' attempts at transformative growth typically spring from product or technology innovations. Their efforts are often characterized by prolonged development cycles and fitful attempts to find a market. As the Apple iPod story that opened this article suggests, truly transformative businesses are never exclusively about the discovery and commercialization of a great technology. Their success comes from enveloping the new technology in an appropriate, powerful business model.

Bob Higgins, the founder and general partner of Highland Capital Partners, has seen his share of venture success and failure in his 20 years in the industry. He sums up the importance and power of business model innovation this way: "I think historically where we [venture capitalists] fail is when we back technology. Where we succeed is when we back new business models."

Originally published in December 2008. Reprint RO812C

The New M&A Playbook

by Clayton M. Christensen, Richard Alton,
Curtis Rising, and Andrew Waldeck

WHEN A CEO WANTS TO BOOST CORPORATE performance or jump-start long-term growth, the thought of acquiring another company can be extraordinarily seductive. Indeed, companies spend more than $2 trillion on acquisitions every year. Yet study after study puts the failure rate of mergers and acquisitions somewhere between 70% and 90%. A lot of researchers have tried to explain those abysmal statistics, usually by analyzing the *attributes* of deals that worked and those that didn't. What's lacking, we believe, is a robust theory that identifies the *causes* of those successes and failures.

Here we propose such a theory. In a nutshell, it is this: So many acquisitions fall short of expectations because executives incorrectly match candidates to the strategic purpose of the deal, failing to distinguish between deals that might improve current operations and those that could dramatically transform the company's growth prospects. As a result, companies too often pay the wrong price and integrate the acquisition in the wrong way.

To state that theory less formally, there are two reasons to acquire a company, which executives often confuse. The first, most common one is to boost your company's current performance—to help you hold on to a premium position, on the one hand, or to cut costs, on the other. An acquisition that delivers those benefits almost never changes the company's trajectory, in large part because investors anticipate and therefore discount the performance improvements. For this kind of deal, CEOs are often unrealistic about how much of a boost to expect, pay too much for the acquisition, and don't understand how to integrate it.

The second, less familiar reason to acquire a company is to reinvent your business model and thereby fundamentally redirect your company. Almost nobody understands how to identify the best targets to achieve that goal, how much to pay for them, and how or whether to integrate them. Yet they are the ones most likely to confound investors and pay off spectacularly.

In this article, we explore the implications of our theory in order to better guide executives in selecting, pricing, and integrating acquisitions and thus dramatically increase their success rate. The first step is to understand at a very basic level what it means for one company to buy another.

What Are We Acquiring?

The success or failure of an acquisition lies in the nuts and bolts of integration. To foresee how integration will play out, we must be able to describe exactly what we are buying.

The best way to do that, we've found, is to think of the target in terms of its business model. As we define it, a business model consists of four interdependent elements that create and deliver value. The first is the customer value proposition: an offering that helps customers do an important job more effectively, conveniently, or affordably than the alternatives. The second element is the profit formula, made up of a revenue model and a cost structure that specify how the company generates profit and the cash required to sustain operations. The third element is the resources—such as employees, customers, technology, products, facilities, and cash—companies use to deliver the customer value proposition. The fourth is processes such as manufacturing, R&D, budgeting, and sales. (For more on this business model construct, see Mark W. Johnson, Clayton M.

Idea in Brief

Most M&As fail. That's because most acquirers don't know how to think systematically about what they're buying and what it might do for them. There is a better way.

If you want to extend your business but not fundamentally change how you compete, you should buy a company with resources that will strengthen your firm. Fold those resources into your existing business and eventually let the acquired business die. But be careful!

Acquirers in this situation usually overpay.

To reinvent your business, you'll need a new business model to complement, extend, or replace your own.

Plug your best resources into the new company, including the technology and capital it needs to grow. Pay liberally: Successful new business models make a lot of money.

Christensen, and Henning Kagermann, "Reinventing Your Business Model," later in this volume.)

Under the right circumstances, one of those elements—resources—can be extracted from an acquired company and plugged into the parent's business model. That's because resources exist apart from the company (the firm could disappear tomorrow, but its resources would still exist). We call such deals "leverage my business model" (LBM) acquisitions.

A company can't, however, routinely plug other elements of an acquisition's business model into its own, or vice versa. Profit formulas and processes don't exist apart from the organization, and they rarely survive its dissolution. But a company can buy another firm's business model, operate it separately, and use it as a platform for transformative growth. We call that a "reinvent my business model" (RBM) acquisition. As we shall see, there is far more growth potential in purchasing other companies' business models than in purchasing their resources.

Executives often believe they can achieve extraordinary returns by acquiring another firm's resources and so pay far too much. Alternatively, they walk away from potentially transformative deals in the mistaken belief that the acquisition is overpriced, or they destroy the value of a high-growth business model by trying to integrate it into their own. To understand why these mistakes are so common and how to avoid them, let's explore in more detail how acquisitions can achieve the two goals mentioned earlier:

- improving current performance
- reinventing a business model.

Boosting Current Performance

A general manager's first task is to deliver the short-term results investors expect through the effective operation of the business. Investors rarely reward managers for those results, but they punish stock values ruthlessly if management falls short. So companies turn to LBM acquisitions to improve the output of their profit formulas.

A successful LBM acquisition enables the parent either to command higher prices or to reduce costs. That sounds simple enough, but the conditions under which an acquisition's resources can help a company accomplish either goal are remarkably specific.

Acquiring resources to command premium prices. The surest way to command a price premium is to improve a product or service that's still developing—in other words, one whose customers are willing to pay for better functionality. Companies routinely do this by purchasing improved components that are compatible with their own products. If such components are not available, then acquiring the needed technology and talent—usually in the form of intellectual property and the scientists and engineers who are creating it—can be a faster route to product improvement than internal development.

Apple's $278 million purchase of chip designer P.A. Semi in 2008 is an example of just such an acquisition. Apple historically had procured its microprocessors from independent suppliers. But as competition with other mobile-device makers increased the competitive importance of battery life, it became difficult to optimize power consumption unless the processors were designed specifically for

Can This Acquisition Help You Command Premium Prices?

WHAT ARE the critical measures of performance that customers value in your product (speed, durability, functionality)?

WOULD MOST customers be willing to pay more if you improved the product on those measures? (Do they value the extra speed, longevity, or functionality enough to pay more for it?)

CAN THE resources of the acquired company substantially improve your product in ways that customers would pay more for?

Apple's products. This meant that to sustain its price premium, Apple needed to purchase the technology and talent to develop an in-house chip design capability—a move that made perfect sense.

Cisco has relied on acquisitions for similar reasons. Because its proprietary product architectures continue to push the leading edge of performance, the company has acquired small high-tech firms and plugged their technologies and engineers into its product development process. (See the sidebar "Can This Acquisition Help You Command Premium Prices?")

Acquiring resources to lower costs. When announcing an acquisition, executives nearly always promise that it will lower costs. In reality, a resource acquisition accomplishes that in only a few scenarios—generally, when the acquiring company has high fixed costs, which allow it to scale up profitably.

Whether they are called "roll ups," "consolidation of shrinking industries," or "natural resource transactions," these deals all succeed in the same way: The parent plugs certain resources from the acquisition into its existing model, jettisoning the rest of the acquired model and shutting down, laying off, or selling redundant resources. The performance boost results from using the target's resources in such a way that scale economics can drive down costs.

Here's a simple example: Many New England homes are heated with oil in the winter. Oil retailers typically make monthly deliveries.

A Word about Conglomeration

THERE IS ONE CATEGORY OF DEAL MAKING NOT ADDRESSED HERE: acquisitions that build or optimize the parent company's portfolio of businesses. Leveraged buyouts by private equity firms are the most prominent example of this kind of deal. Although many LBO firms try to add value to their portfolio companies through operational improvements, much of the actual value to the acquirer is created by the use of leverage and the accompanying tax shield. These deals more closely resemble a stock purchase than a strategic acquisition. Other investors, such as Warren Buffett of Berkshire Hathaway and Ian Cumming of Leucadia National, purchase businesses for similar reasons, albeit with much less leverage. Large conglomerate acquisitions are sometimes made to diversify the parent's portfolio rather than for strategic fit with its current businesses. GE's acquisition of NBC arguably fits this description. We do not question the value of such acquisitions, which can be considerable. But they are not the kind that can have a direct and transformative impact on a company's business model.

If one retailer buys a competitor that operates in the same neighborhoods, the parent is essentially buying the competitor's customers and can eliminate the duplicate fixed costs of two trucks that serve neighboring customers. Here the critical acquired resource is not the trucks or drivers, which the company does not need to serve the new customers; it is the customers themselves, and they are plug-compatible with the parent's resources, processes, and profit formula. That's why the deal will lower the acquirer's costs.

But if the heating oil company purchased a similar firm in a different city, the acquisition would replicate the parent's cost position in a new geographic area, not reduce it in either one. There might be some overhead efficiencies, but costs would be lowered far less than in the previous example because the oil retailer would need the acquired company's trucks to service its new customers.

One sees scale-enhancing resource acquisitions like the same-neighborhood oil company deal when a pharmaceutical company acquires another so that it can carry the acquired products through its high-fixed-cost sales channel, or when ArcelorMittal buys competing steel companies, transfers production to utilize excess capacity in its most-efficient mills, and then shuts down redundant mills.

Can This Acquisition Help You Lower Costs?

PREDICTING WHETHER THE RESOURCES of a prospective acquisition will improve the output of your company's business model, and so lower costs, is mainly a matter of assessing how compatible they are with your company's resources and processes.

RESOURCES	PROCESSES
WILL THE acquisition's products fit into my product catalog without creating confusion?	**CAN THE** acquisition's offering be sold according to our sales cycle?
DO ITS customers buy products like ours, and vice versa?	**CAN MY** people readily service the acquired customers?
CAN THE output of the acquisition's factories be used with minimal adjustment by our supply chain and distributors?	**CAN ITS** products be produced in our factories, and vice versa?
DO OUR salespeople have the skills to sell the acquisition's products? Will they be excited to sell them?	**WILL THE** quality of its offerings be enhanced by our rules for managing procurement, IT systems, and quality control systems?

If the resources of the target are compatible with your resources and processes, the acquisition will most likely improve the resource velocity of your profit formula—that is, there is a good chance it will improve turnover or utilization of assets and fixed costs.

Oil and natural gas company Anadarko's 2006 acquisition of Kerr-McGee followed the same pattern. What made Kerr-McGee attractive was the adjacency of its oil fields to Anadarko's. The combined firm could operate those fields with the same network of pipelines, support ships, and other fixed operating assets. Had Kerr-McGee's fields been in the North Atlantic and Anadarko's in the Gulf of Mexico, Anadarko would have had to maintain independent fixed-cost networks to support both operations. This would have resulted only in overhead efficiencies and potentially greater managerial complexity.

To work out whether a potential resource acquisition will help lower your costs, you must determine whether the acquisition's resources are compatible with your own and with your processes (see the sidebar "Can This Acquisition Help You Lower Costs?") and then determine whether scale increases will actually have the desired effect.

For companies in industries where fixed costs represent a large percentage of total costs, increasing scale through acquisitions results in substantial cost savings, in the same way that the oil company could lower its costs by buying a local competitor. But in industries where cost-competitiveness can be reached at relatively low levels of market share, a company growing beyond that does not reduce its cost position but replicates it, as would a heating oil company that purchased customers in a different city. (See the exhibit "When will increased scale lower costs?") In the polyester fabric industry, for example, once a firm is big enough to fully utilize a state-of-the-art air-jet loom, any growth in volume requires the producer to buy another loom. For companies whose cost structures are dominated by variable costs, resource acquisitions typically yield only minimal improvements to the profit formula.

Similarly, the benefits of scale are most substantial in operating categories that have a high percentage of fixed costs, such as manufacturing, distribution, and sales. Acquisitions that are justified by economies of scale in administrative costs such as purchasing, human resources, or legal services often have disappointing effects on the profit formula. When the *New York Times* acquired the *Boston Globe*, for example, there were few operating synergies (reporters and printing were by necessity separate). The administrative overlaps in areas like HR and finance were not enough to make this a good deal.

As a general rule, the impact of an LBM acquisition on the acquirer's share price will be apparent within one year, because the market understands the full potential of both businesses before the acquisition and has had enough time to assess the outcome of

When will increased scale lower costs?

If fixed costs represent a large percentage of your total costs, you can reap substantial savings by increasing scale. But if your costs are more variable than fixed, scale increases may require new overhead investments and so deliver minimal savings.

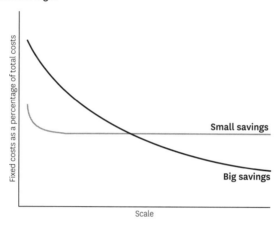

the integration and any synergies that may arise. Investors are often much less optimistic than CEOs about LBM deals, and history generally proves them right: The best-case result is a jump in share price to a new plateau. Some managers hold out hope that LBM acquisitions can unlock unexpected growth, but as we will see, they are likely to be disappointed.

The temptation of one-stop shopping. A word of warning is in order for companies seeking to boost current performance through LBM deals aimed at acquiring new customers: All the successful examples we've identified involve selling "acquired" customers the products they were already buying. Acquisitions made for the purpose of cross-selling products succeed only occasionally.

Why? Let's say Clayton Christensen is a typical shopper, who buys both consumer electronics and hardware. Wouldn't Walmart, which carries both product categories, have a better chance of winning his business than Best Buy, which sells only consumer electronics, or

Home Depot, which sells only hardware? In a word, no. That's because Clay needs to buy electronics just before birthdays and holidays, whereas he needs to buy hardware on Saturday mornings, when he intends to repair something at home. Because these two jobs-to-be-done arise at different times, the fact that Walmart can sell him both kinds of products does not give it an advantage over the specialists. Typical shopper Clay does, however, buy gasoline and junk food at the same time—when he's on a road trip. Hence, we have seen a convergence of convenience stores and gas stations. In other words, an acquisition whose rationale is to sell a variety of products to new customers will succeed only if customers need to buy those products at the same time and in the same place.

More than once, ambitious executives, such as Sanford Weill of Citigroup fame, have assembled "financial supermarkets," thinking that customers' needs for credit cards, checking accounts, wealth management services, insurance, and stock brokerage could be furnished most efficiently and effectively by the same company. Those efforts have failed, over and over again. Each function fulfills a different job that arises at a different point in a customer's life, so a single source for all of them holds no advantage. Cross-selling in circumstances like these will complicate and confuse, and will rarely reduce sales costs.

Reinventing Your Business Model

The second fundamental task of a general manager is to lay the groundwork for long-term growth by creating new ways of doing business, since the value of existing business models fades as competition and technological progress erode their profit potential. RBM acquisitions help managers tackle that task.

Investors' expectations give executives a strong incentive to embrace the work of reinvention. As Alfred Rappaport and Michael Mauboussin point out in their book *Expectations Investing* (Harvard Business Review Press, 2003), managers quickly learn that it is not earnings growth per se that determines growth in their company's share price—it's growth relative to investors' expectations. A firm's share price represents myriad pieces of information about its predicted performance, synthesized into a single number and discounted into its present value. If managers grow cash flows at the rate the market expects, the firm's share price will grow only at its cost of capital, because those expectations have already been factored into its current share price. To persistently create shareholder value at a greater rate, managers must do something that investors haven't already taken into account—and they must do it again and again.

Acquiring a disruptive business model. The most reliable sources of unexpected growth in revenues and margins are disruptive products and business models. Disruptive companies are those whose initial products are simpler and more affordable than the established players' offerings. They secure their foothold in the low end of the market and then move to higher-performance, higher-margin products, market tier by market tier. Although investment analysts can see a company's potential in the market tier where it's currently positioned, they fail to foresee how a disruptor will move upmarket as its offerings improve. So they persistently underestimate the growth potential of disruptive companies.

To understand how that works, consider Nucor, an operator of steel minimills, which back in the 1970s developed a radically simpler and less costly way to make steel than the big integrated steelmakers of the day. Initially, Nucor made only concrete reinforcing bar (rebar), the simplest and lowest-margin of all steel products. Analysts valued Nucor according to the size of the rebar market and the profits Nucor could earn in it. But the pursuit of profit drove Nucor to develop further capabilities, and as it invaded subsequent product tiers, commanding higher and higher margins from its low-cost manufacturing technique, analysts kept having to revisit their estimates of the company's addressable market—and hence its growth.

As a result, Nucor's share price fairly exploded, as the exhibit "Why disruptive businesses are worth so much" demonstrates. From 1983 to 1994, Nucor's stock appreciated at a 27% compounded

Why disruptive businesses are worth so much

As nucor moves from low-end to high-end segments...

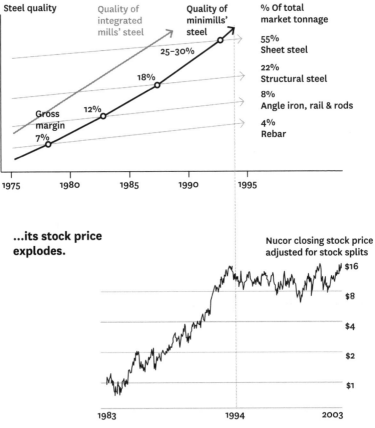

...its stock price explodes.

What produces a dramatic increase in a company's share price? Growth that investors weren't predicting. As Nucor developed revolutionary approaches to steel making, the company was able to enter increasingly larger segments of the steel market—each time prompting investors to reconsider Nucor's share price. Once there were no new markets to conquer, the company's share price leveled off.

Source: Bloomberg

annual rate, as analysts continually realized that they had underestimated the markets the company could address. By 1994, Nucor was in the top market tier, and analysts caught up with its growth potential. Even though sales continued to increase handsomely, that accurate understanding, or "discountability," caused Nucor's share price to level off. If executives had wanted the company's share price to keep appreciating at rates in excess of analysts' expectations, they would have had to continue to create or acquire disruptive businesses.

A company that acquires a disruptive business model can achieve spectacular results. Take, for example, information technology giant EMC's acquisition of VMware, whose software enabled IT departments to run multiple "virtual servers" on a single machine, replacing server vendors' pricey hardware solution with a lower-cost software one. Although this offering was disruptive to server vendors, it was complementary to EMC, giving the storage hardware vendor greater reach into its customers' data rooms. When EMC acquired VMware, for $635 million in cash, VMware's revenues were just $218 million. With a disruptive wind at its back, VMware's growth exploded: Annual revenues reached $2.6 billion in 2010. Currently, EMC's stake in VMware is worth more than $28 billion, a stunning 44-fold increase of its initial investment.

Johnson & Johnson's Medical Devices & Diagnostics division provides another example of how reinventing a business model through acquisition can boost growth from average to exceptional. From 1992 through 2001, the division's portfolio of products performed adequately, growing revenues at an annual rate of 3%. But during the same period, the division acquired four small but disruptive business models that ignited outsize growth. Together these RBM acquisitions grew 41% annually over this period, fundamentally changing the division's growth trajectory. (See the sidebar "Can This Acquisition Change Your Company's Growth Trajectory?")

Acquiring to decommoditize. One of the most effective ways to use RBM acquisitions is as a defense against commoditization. As we have described previously in this magazine, the dynamics of commoditization tend to follow a predictable pattern (see

Can This Acquisition Change Your Company's Growth Trajectory?

IS THE acquired company's product or service simpler and more affordable than the established players' offerings?

DO THIS simplicity and affordability enable more people to own and use the product or service? Is it good enough to suit the needs of a variety of customers?

CAN THE acquired company's business model scale upmarket to yield a stream of progressively higher-capability products and services?

DO established players find the company's offering profitable enough to replicate, or is the company playing in low-end markets that incumbents are content to ignore?

DOES THE acquired company reposition you to capture the most attractive (future) profits in the industry's value chain?

Clayton M. Christensen, Michael Raynor, and Matt Verlinden, "Skate to Where the Money Will Be," later in this volume. Over time, the most profitable point in the value chain shifts as proprietary, integrated offerings metamorphose into modular, undifferentiated ones. The innovative companies supplying the components start to capture the most attractive margins in the chain.

If a firm finds itself being commoditized in this way, acquisitions won't improve the output of its profit formula. In fact, nothing will. Firms in this situation should instead migrate to "where the profits will be"—the point in the value chain that will capture the best margins in the future. Right now, the business models of major pharmaceutical companies are floundering for a host of reasons, including their inability to fill new-product pipelines and the obsolescence of the direct-to-doctor sales model. Industry leaders like Pfizer, GSK, and Merck have tried to boost the output of their troubled business models by buying and integrating the products and pipeline resources of competing drugmakers. But in the wake of such acquisitions, Pfizer's share price plummeted 40%. A far better strategy would be to focus on the place in the value chain that is becoming decommoditized: the management of clinical trials, which are now an integral part of the drug research process and so a critical capability for pharmaceutical companies. Despite this, most drugmakers have been outsourcing their clinical trials to contract research organizations such as Covance and Quintiles, better positioning those companies in the value chain. Acquiring those organizations, or a disruptive drugmaker like Dr. Reddy's Laboratories, would help reinvent big pharma's collapsing business model.

Paying the Right Price

Given our assertion that RBM acquisitions most effectively raise the rate of value creation for shareholders, it's ironic that acquirers typically underpay for those acquisitions and overpay for LBM ones.

The stacks of M&A literature are littered with warnings about paying too much, and for good reason. Many an executive has been caught up in deal fever and paid more for an LBM deal than could be justified by cost synergies. For that kind of deal, it's crucial to determine the target's worth by calculating the impact on profits from the acquisition. If an acquirer pays less than that, the stock price will increase, but only to a slightly higher plateau, with a gentle upward slope representing the company's weighted-average cost of capital, which for most firms is about 8%. In contrast, consider the exhibit "How the market rewards disruptors," which charts the average earnings multiple of 37 companies we've determined to be disruptive in the 10 years after they went public. Annual P/E ratios for this group are far higher than historical levels, leading analysts to believe their shares were overpriced. Yet investors who purchased at the time of the IPO and held the stock for 10 years realized an astounding 46% annual return, indicating that the shares were persistently underpriced, even at these "high" multiples.

Analysts charged with determining the right price for a company's shares work hard to find appropriate comparables. For LBM acquisitions, the correct comparables are companies that make similar products in similar industries. For RBM acquisitions, however, such comparables make disruptive companies seem overpriced, deterring

---

How the market rewards disruptors

High price/earnings ratios (which indicate a high share price relative to net income or profits) in a sample of 37 disruptive companies led analysts to believe their shares were overpriced at the time of their IPOs. The extraordinary performance of these companies in the market, however, suggests that their shares were in fact persistently underpriced.

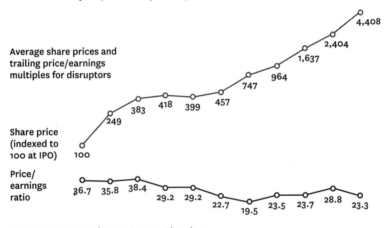

Average share prices and trailing price/earnings multiples for disruptors

Share price (indexed to 100 at IPO)

Price/earnings ratio

Sources: Compustat, Thomson Reuters, Bloomberg

---

companies from pursuing the very acquisitions they need for reinvention. In reality, the right comparables for disruptive companies are other disruptors, regardless of industry.

Ultimately, the "right" price for an acquisition is not something that can be set by the seller, far less by an investment banker looking to sell to the highest bidder. The right price can be determined only by the buyer, since it depends on what purpose the acquisition will serve.

Avoiding Integration Mistakes

Your approach to integration should be determined almost entirely by the type of acquisition you've made. If you buy another company for the purpose of improving your current business model's effectiveness, you should generally dissolve the acquired model as its resources are folded into your operations. That's what Cisco does with the great majority of its technology acquisitions. (There are certainly exceptions: An acquired process, for instance, is sometimes so valuable or distinct that it substitutes for or is added to the acquirer's.) But if you buy a company for its business model, it's important to keep the model intact, most commonly by operating it separately. That's what Best Buy did with Geek Squad, running its high-touch, higher-cost service model as a separate business alongside its low-margin, low-touch retail operation. Likewise, VMware's server-focused business model was distinct enough from EMC's storage model that EMC chose not to integrate VMware very closely. EMC's original business model continued to perform well, but the addition of VMware's disruptive business model allowed EMC to grow at an exceptional rate.

Failing to understand where the value resides in what's been bought, and therefore integrating incorrectly, has caused some of the biggest disasters in acquisitions history. Daimler's 1998 acquisition of Chrysler for $36 billion is a quintessential example. Although the purchase of one car company by another looks like a classic resource acquisition, that was a fatal way to look at it. From about 1988 to 1998, Chrysler had aggressively modularized its products, outsourcing the subsystems from which its cars could be assembled to its tier-one suppliers. This so simplified its design processes that Chrysler could cut its design cycle from five years to two (compared with about six years at Daimler) and could design a car at one-fifth the overhead cost that Daimler required. As a result, during this period Chrysler introduced a series of very popular models and gained nearly a point of market share every year.

When Daimler's acquisition of Chrysler was announced, analysts began the "synergies" drumbeat—and Daimler responded that integrating the companies would strip out $8 billion in "redundant" costs. But when Daimler folded Chrysler's resources (brands, dealers, factories, and technology) into its operations, the real value of the acquisition (Chrysler's speedy processes and lean profit formula) disappeared, and with it the basis for Chrysler's success. Daimler would have done far better to preserve Chrysler's business model as a separate entity.

Companies rightly turn to acquisitions to meet goals they can't achieve internally. But there is no magic in buying another company. Companies can make acquisitions that allow them to command higher prices, but only in the same way they could have raised prices all along—by improving products that are not yet good enough for the majority of their customers. Similarly, they can make acquisitions to cut costs by using excess capacity in their resources and processes to serve new customers—but again, only in the same way they could have by finding new customers on their own. And companies can acquire new business models to serve as platforms for transformative growth—just as they could if they developed new business models in-house. At the end of the day, the decision to acquire is a question of whether it is faster and more economical to buy something that you could, given enough time and resources, make yourself.

Every day, the wrong companies are purchased for the wrong purpose, the wrong measures of value are applied in pricing the deals, and the wrong elements are integrated into the wrong business models. Sounds like a mess—and it has been a mess. But it need not be. We hope that the next time an investment banker knocks on your door with a guaranteed fee for himself and the acquisition of a lifetime for you, you'll be able to predict with greater accuracy whether the company on offer is a dream deal or a debacle.

Originally published in March 2011. Reprint R1103B

Skate to Where the Money Will Be

by Clayton M. Christensen, Michael Raynor, and Matthew Verlinden

WHEN IBM DECIDED TO OUTSOURCE ITS operating system and processor chips in the early 1980s, it was, or appeared to be, at the top of its game. It owned 70% of the entire mainframe market, controlled 95% of its profits, and had long dominated the industry. Yet disaster famously ensued, as Intel and Microsoft subsequently captured the lion's share of the computer industry's profits, and Big Blue entered a decade of decline.

It's easy to look back and ask, "What were they *thinking?*" but, in truth, IBM's decision fit well with prevailing orthodoxies, particularly with the idea that companies should outsource all but their core competencies—that is, sell off or outsource any function that another company could do better or cheaper than it could. Indeed, at the time, many observers hailed IBM's move as a masterstroke of strategy, forward-looking and astute.

Of course it turned out not to be, but what lessons should we draw from IBM's spectacular mistake? They're far from clear. It's easy to say, "Don't outsource the thing that's going to make lots of money *next,*" but existing models of industry competitiveness offer very little help in predicting where, in an industry's value chain, future profitability will be most attractive. Executives and investors all wish they could be like Wayne Gretzky, with his uncanny ability to sense where the puck is about to go. But many companies discover

The Disruptive Technologies Model

THE DISRUPTIVE TECHNOLOGIES MODEL CONTRASTS the pace of technological progress with customers' ability to use that progress. According to the model, there are two types of performance trajectories in every market. One trajectory, depicted by the shaded area, shows how much improvement in a product or service customers can absorb over time. The other trajectory, shown by the solid lines, depicts the improvement that innovators in the industry generate as they introduce new and enhanced products.

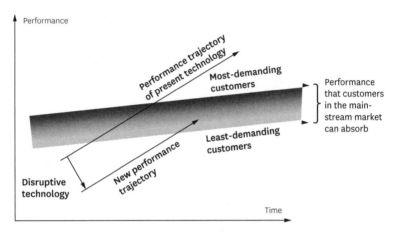

Almost always, this second trajectory—the pace of technological innovation—outstrips the ability of customers in a given tier of the market to absorb it. This creates the potential for innovative companies to enter the lower tiers of the market with "disruptive technologies"—cheaper, simpler, more convenient products or services. Almost always, the leading companies are so absorbed with upmarket innovations addressed to their most sophisticated and profitable customers that they miss the disruptive innovations. Disruptive technologies have caused many of history's best companies to plunge into crisis and fail.

that once they get to the place where the money is, there's very little of it left to go around.

Over the past six years, we've been studying the evolution of industry value chains, and we've seen a recurring pattern that goes a long way toward explaining why companies so often make strategic errors in choosing where to focus their efforts and resources. Understanding

Idea in Brief

As hockey great Wayne Gretzky once said, the key to winning is skating *first* to where the puck will be *next*. Business success is similar. We all want to go where the greatest profits *will* be—but by the time most of us get there, the "puck" has moved on.

Consider IBM: Riding high in the early 1980s, the company clung to where the money *had* been—computer-system design/assembly—outsourcing its processor chips and operating system to Intel and Microsoft. A 10-year decline followed, as Intel and Microsoft—navigating to where the money *would* be—captured industry profits.

How to avoid similar disaster? Understand how industries evolve. Then use your insights to:

- Predict profit migration as your industry matures.

- Focus resources on activities that are about to generate substantial profits.

the pattern helps answer some of the enduring questions that IBM's leaders, and thousands of others before and since, grappled with: Where will attractive profits be earned in the value chain of the future? Under what circumstances will integrated corporations wield powerful competitive advantages? What changes in circumstances will shift competitive advantage to specialized, nonintegrated companies? What causes an industry to fragment? How can a dominant, integrated player determine what to outsource and what to hold on to as its industry begins to break into pieces? How can new entrants figure out where to target their efforts to maximize profitability?

The pattern we observed arises out of a key tenet of the concept of "disruptive technologies"—that the pace of technological progress generated by established players inevitably outstrips customers' ability to absorb it, creating opportunity for up-starts to displace incumbents. This model has long been used to predict how an industry will change as customers' needs are exceeded. (See the sidebar "The Disruptive Technologies Model.") Building on that ground, this new theory provides a useful gauge for measuring not only where competition will arise under those circumstances but also where, in an industry's shifting value chain, the money will be made in the future.

The implications of our theory will surprise many readers because, if we're right, the money will not be made where most

Idea in Practice

How Value Chains Evolve

As industries and their products mature, value chains evolve predictably:

Stage 1: A Tight Fit. Early products' functionalities do not yet meet key customers' needs (e.g., the first mainframe computers weren't powerful or fast). Companies compete on performance, making the highest-quality products for their most demanding—and profitable—customers.

Firms also push technological frontiers—developing and combining product components more efficiently, using interdependent, proprietary product architectures. Large, established, vertically integrated companies dominate, because all their units communicate under one roof. Products for end-users constitute the most profitable point on the value chain.

Example: Telephone companies still dominate in high-speed Internet access via phone lines—because too many unpredictable interdependencies exist between DSL providers and phone companies. By spanning the entire value chain, incumbent phone companies provide more reliable service.

Stage 2: Going to Pieces. As companies stretch to meet their most demanding customers' needs, product performance overshoots *mainstream* consumers' needs. Disruptive companies enter this less demanding market, displacing incumbents by quickly delivering flexible, customized, and cheaper products.

Example: In the 1990s, computer-industry overshooting shifted competitiveness to speed, convenience,

companies are headed, as they busily outsource exactly the things they should be holding on to and hold on to precisely the things they should unload. But we'll get to that later . . .

A Tight Fit

Companies compete differently at different stages of a product's evolution. In the early days, when a product's functionality does not yet meet the needs of key customers, companies compete on the basis of product performance. Later, as the underlying technology improves and mainstream customers' needs are met, companies are and customization. Dell Computer's well-timed business model—featuring outsourced subsystems, custom assembly, quick delivery, and competitive prices—garnered astounding success.

Fuzzy Links

As an industry continues to mature, the most profitable point along the value chain shifts from end-use products to components and subsystems—which still have technologically *interdependent* internal architectures.

Rather than redesign everything, successful companies at this stage mix and match the best components from top suppliers to meet customers' needs—creating interdependent links between components and subsystems.

Who Wins?

When products' architectures are interdependent and proprietary, competitors can't easily copy them. Therefore, companies who control the *interdependent links* in their industry's value chain dominate.

How to control those links? As your industry matures and fragments, don't spin off or outsource asset-intensive businesses to companies that will create subsystems with progressively more interdependent architectures. Instead, flexibly couple and decouple operations. Learning from earlier mistakes, IBM now chops up its integrated value chain—selling its technology, components, and subsystems in the open market—and has created a high-end systems-integration business. Skating to value-chain points requiring complex, nonstandard integration, IBM now earns impressive profits.

forced to compete on the basis of convenience, customization, price, and flexibility. These different bases of competition call for very different organizational structures at both the company and industry levels.

When products aren't yet good enough for mainstream customers, competitive pressures force engineers to focus on wringing the best possible performance out of each succeeding product generation by developing and combining proprietary components in ever more efficient ways. They can't assemble off-the-shelf components using standard interfaces because that would force them to back away from the frontier of what's technologically possible. When the product is not good enough, backing off from the best you can do spells competitive trouble. To make the highest-performing products possible, then, companies typically need to adopt interdependent, proprietary product architectures.

During the early days of the computer industry, for example, when mainframes were not yet powerful or fast enough to satisfy mainstream customers' needs, an independent contract manufacturer assembling machines from suppliers' components could not have survived because the way the machines were designed depended on the way they were manufactured and vice versa. Nor could an independent supplier of operating systems, core memory, or logic circuitry have survived because these key subsystems had to be designed interdependently, too.

When the product isn't good enough, in other words, being an integrated company is critical to success. As the most integrated company during the early era of the computer industry, IBM dominated its world. Ford and General Motors, as the most integrated automakers, dominated their industry during the era when cars were not good enough. For the same reasons, RCA, Xerox, AT&T, Alcoa, Standard Oil, and U.S. Steel dominated their industries at similar stages. Their products were based on the sorts of proprietary, interdependent value chains that are necessary when pushing the frontier of what is possible.

When a nonintegrated company tries to compete under these circumstances, it usually fails. Stitching together a system with other "partner" companies is extremely difficult when the subsystems and expertise those companies provide are interdependent. We could offer numerous historical examples, but there are plenty of illustrations from industries that are still emerging. In the late 1990s, for example, many nonintegrated companies attempted to offer high-speed DSL access to the Internet over phone lines operated by telephone companies. Most of these attempts failed. Many believe that low prices for DSL service that were rooted in regulatory peculiarities of the Telecommunications Act of 1996 are what drove the competitive local exchange carriers toward bankruptcy. This was only the proximate cause of their demise, however. The fundamental issue is that at this point in the industry's evolution,

DSL technology isn't good enough yet, and there are, as a result, too many unpredictable interdependencies between what focused DSL providers need to do and what the telephone companies must do in response. The incumbent phone companies' capacity to span the whole value chain has been a powerful advantage. They understand their own network architectures and can consequently offer service more quickly, with fewer concerns about the unintended consequences of reconfiguring their own central-office facilities. Regulatory mandates cannot decouple an industry at an interdependent interface. As long as DSL service is not good enough to satisfy most users, the integrated telephone companies will be able to provide better, more reliable service than nonintegrated competitors.

Going to Pieces

Product performance almost always improves beyond the needs of the general consumer, as companies stretch to meet the needs of the most demanding (and most profitable) customers. When technological progress overshoots what mainstream customers can make use of, companies that want to win the business of the overserved customers in less-demanding tiers of the market are forced to change the way they compete. They must bring more flexible products to market faster and customize their products to meet the needs of customers in ever smaller market niches.

To compete on these new dimensions, companies must design modular products, in which the interfaces between components and subsystems are clearly specified. Ultimately, these interfaces coalesce into industry standards. Modular architectures help companies introduce new products faster because subsystems can be improved without having to redesign everything. Companies can mix and match the best components from the best suppliers to respond to the specific needs of individual customers. Although standard interfaces invariably force compromises in system performance, competitors aiming at overserved customers can comfortably trade off some performance to achieve the benefits of speed and flexibility.

Once a modular architecture and the requisite industry standards have been defined, integration is no longer crucial to a company's success. In fact, it becomes a competitive disadvantage in terms of speed, flexibility, and price, and the industry tends to dis-integrate as a consequence. The exhibit "The dis-integration of the computer industry" illustrates how this happened in that field. During its early decades, the dominant companies were integrated across most value-chain links because competitive conditions mandated integration. As the personal computer disrupted the industry, however, it was as if the industry got pushed through a bologna slicer. The dominant, integrated companies were displaced by specialists that competed in horizontal strata within the value chain.

This shift explains why Dell Computer was so successful in the 1990s. Dell did not succeed because its products were better than those of competitors IBM, Compaq, and the like. Rather, overshooting triggered a shift in the basis of competition to speed, convenience,

The dis-integration of the computer industry

Mainframes and minicomputers were never good enough or fast enough or cheap enough to create a mass market and were therefore always the province of large, integrated players who built their machines from their own proprietary designs and components. The PC, though, very quickly became good enough for the average consumer, giving rise to an army of specialized players.

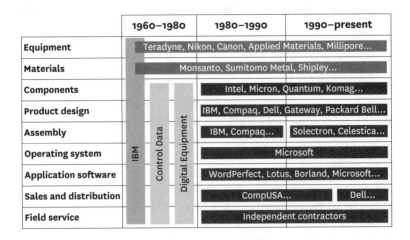

	1960–1980	1980–1990	1990–present
Equipment	Teradyne, Nikon, Canon, Applied Materials, Millipore...		
Materials	Monsanto, Sumitomo Metal, Shipley...		
Components		Intel, Micron, Quantum, Komag...	
Product design		IBM, Compaq, Dell, Gateway, Packard Bell...	
Assembly		IBM, Compaq...	Solectron, Celestica...
Operating system	IBM / Control Data / Digital Equipment	Microsoft	
Application software		WordPerfect, Lotus, Borland, Microsoft...	
Sales and distribution		CompUSA...	Dell...
Field service		Independent contractors	

and customization, and Dell's business model was a perfect match for that environment. Customers were delighted to buy computers with outsourced subsystems, custom-assembled to their own specifications and delivered incredibly quickly at competitive prices. This also explains how Cisco, with its disruptive router and its noninte-grated business model, bested more integrated competitors like Lucent in the market for telecommunications equipment.

Fuzzy Links

The careful reader will have noticed that the interfaces between stages in the value chain are central to our argument—both to the forces that support integration in the early years of an industry and to those that ultimately pull an industry apart into component pieces. They'll become even more important when we move on to profitability flows in a moment. So let's look more closely at what we mean by "the interfaces between components and subsystems."

Say a company is considering whether it's feasible to procure a subsystem from a supplier or partner rather than make it in-house. Three conditions must be met. First, managers need to know what to specify—which attributes of the item they're procuring are crucial and which are not. Second, they must be able to measure those attributes so they can verify that they have received what they need. Third, there can't be any unpredictable interdependencies: They need to understand how the subsystem will perform with the other pieces of the system so that it can be used with predictable effect. These conditions—specifiability, verifiability, and predictability—are prerequisites to modular designs that enable companies to work efficiently with suppliers and partners. They constitute what economists would term "sufficient information" for an efficient market to emerge for a particular component or subsystem.

Typically, when product performance has become more than good enough, the technologies being used are mature enough for these conditions to be met—facilitating the decoupling of the value chain. It is when performance is *not* good enough that new technologies are used in new ways—and in those circumstances the conditions of specifiability, verifiability, and predictability often are not

Management Education—Ripe for Dis-Integration

FEW INDUSTRIES ARE EXEMPT from the forces of disruption and dis-integration, management education included. This industry is changing, and whether these changes prove to be a boon or a bane to leading schools of management depends on how they address these forces.

At the top of the heap, big-name business schools offer top-tier MBA students a premium, expensive product. It's worth it: Graduates easily command starting salaries of $130,000 or more, and they're in high demand. True to the model, the architecture of top-tier MBA programs is interdependent. Their premise is that future managers can't understand marketing, for example, unless they study product development, and they can't study product development without studying manufacturing, and so on. The programs are also integrated in the sense that the faculty members do everything, soup to nuts: conduct research, writes cases and articles, design courses, and teach.

But the familiar pattern of overshooting and subsequent modularization is becoming evident. As graduates of these top-tier schools have become more expensive to employ, a significant portion of graduates now take jobs with consulting firms, investment banks, and high-tech start-ups. The established operating companies that historically had been major employers of MBAs increasingly find these graduates to be too expensive to fit into their salary structures and career paths.

Increasingly, those companies, and even some consulting firms, are opting to train their own. They hire people with bachelor's or graduate technical degrees, then help them build managerial skills in formally organized institutions like Motorola University and GE's Crotonville. Other companies have less-structured, but equally extensive, management-training programs. Last year, IBM spent more than $500 million on management training, for example, and announced it would begin selling management education programs to other companies' executives as well.

Like most disruptions, these on-the-job training programs are probably not as good as what they're replacing, at least in the way the elite schools define "good." They're certainly not as thorough, and their students aren't, on average, quite as polished and prepared as the best MBA students. But like other disruptive businesses, they compete on different terms. On-the-job training programs are modular, custom-assembled courses whose content is tailored to specific issues the manager-students face. Managers will take a three-day course on strategic thinking, for instance, then use what they've learned to define a better strategy.

It may not be as comprehensive as an MBA strategy class, but because it's better targeted to the students' immediate needs, it often proves more useful to them and to their employers. And in contrast to the leading schools' integrated structure, on-the-job management education is dis-integrated. Hundreds of specialized companies develop materials; others design courses; still others produce and teach them.

How should the top management schools react? They could, of course, ignore the trend—there won't be a dearth of MBA students anytime soon, and these institutions will likely survive in their current form for years. If they ignore the disruption, though, they will gradually lose influence because the vast majority of learning about management already occurs on the job. A second alternative is to skate to where the money is: to the design and assembly of customized courses for on-the-job training. This is tempting because the custom executive-education market is growing, but it would be hard to compete against the focused, flexible specialists already in that space.

A better idea is to skate to where the money will be—to become the "Intel Inside" of corporate-training programs. That means providing not just single components in the form of cases or articles but rather "subsystems," modules with proprietary internal architectures. These would be predefined sets of cases, articles, news clips, and video materials from which well-defined insights can cumulatively but interdependently be built. Teaching notes that make explicit the connections within these materials—connections that historically have resided only in the intuition of the professors who wrote the materials—would make it simple for a larger set of less well-trained instructors in a corporate setting to do a great job teaching powerful concepts. Companies that design courses could mix and match such materials to address students' needs.

Always, disruption facilitates new waves of growth in an industry because it enables more people to buy and consume. If our model is right, future profits in the growing portions of this industry will come not from the design and assembly of courses, anyway, but from the development of the subsystems that make up those courses. That's where the steep scale economies and differentiated materials should reside. If the leading management schools worked in this way to facilitate their own disruption, they would find they can continue to teach MBA students within their conventional model for the foreseeable future, even as they participate in the growth of the total management education industry—and continue to enjoy much of the profit as well.

met. When sufficient information does not exist at an interface, managerial coordination will always trump market mechanisms, reinforcing the strength of integrated companies.

The evolving structure of the lending industry offers a good example of these forces at work. Integrated banks such as Chase and Deutsche Bank have powerful competitive advantages in the most complex tiers of the lending market. Integration is key to their ability to knit together huge, complex financing packages for sophisticated and demanding global customers. Decisions about whether and how much to lend cannot be made according to fixed formulas and measures; they can only be made through the intuition of experienced lending officers. The high-end bankers who create innovative, complex financial instruments for these customers play a similar role to engineers who push the technological envelope when product functionality is not good enough. In both cases, meeting the needs of the most demanding customers requires that all the constituent parts be under one roof, able to communicate through organizational rather than market mechanisms.

The simpler tiers of the lending market, on the other hand, are being disrupted by innovations in the way credit-worthiness is established—specifically by credit-scoring technology and advances in asset securitization. In these tiers, lenders know and can measure precisely those attributes that determine the likelihood that a borrower will repay a loan. Verifiable information about borrowers— how long they have lived, where they live, how long they have worked, where they work, what their income is, and whether they've paid bills on time—is fed into powerful algorithms, which are used to automate lending decisions. Credit scoring took root in the 1960s in the lowest tier of the market, as department stores began to issue their own credit cards. Then, unfortunately for the big banks, the specialist horde of nonbank institutions moved inexorably upmarket in pursuit of profits—first to general consumer credit-card loans, then to automobile and mortgage loans, and now to small-business loans. True to form, the lending industry in these simpler tiers of the market has largely dis-integrated, as these specialist companies have emerged, each focusing on just a slice of added value.

Where the Money Goes

Clearly, companies competing in an integrated market face very different challenges from those competing in a fragmented market—the ball game changes fundamentally once components become modular and customers' thoughts turn to speed or convenience rather than functionality. Sources of profitability change as well. Our model can help managers, strategists, and investors assess how the power to grab profits is likely to shift in the future. The bedrock principle is this: Those who control the interdependent links in a value chain capture the most profit.

In periods when product functionality is not yet good enough, integrated companies that design and make end-use products typically make the most money, for two reasons. First, the interdependent, proprietary architecture of their products makes differentiation straightforward. Second, the high ratio of fixed to variable costs, which is inherent to the design and manufacture of architecturally interdependent products, creates steep economies of scale. Larger competitors can amortize high fixed costs over greater volume, giving them strong cost advantages over smaller competitors. Making highly differentiated products with strong cost advantages is a license to print money, and lots of it.

Hence IBM, as the most integrated competitor in the mainframe computer industry, made 95% of the industry's profits from just a 70% market share. And from the 1950s through the 1970s, General Motors garnered 80% of the profits from about 55% of the U.S. auto market. Most of IBM's and GM's suppliers, by contrast, survived on subsistence profits year after year.

But when the large integrated players overshoot what their mainstream customers can use, the tables begin to turn. Disruptive competitors begin to move upmarket, and the power to make money shifts away from companies that design and assemble the end-use product toward the back end of the value chain to those companies that supply subsystems with internal architectures that are still technologically interdependent.

A good way to visualize this is to imagine an engineer employed at Compaq whose boss just told her to design a desktop computer better than Dell's, IBM's, or Hewlett-Packard's. How would she do it? When designing and assembling a modular product, your competitors can replicate anything you can do very quickly. And because most of the costs in an outsourcing-intensive business model are variable rather than fixed, there are minimal economies of scale, so that large and small competitors have similar costs. Making an undifferentiated product at undifferentiated costs is a recipe for earning undifferentiated profits.

So, what's our Compaq engineer to do? She'll put pressure on her suppliers to invent faster microprocessors and higher-capacity, lower-cost disk drives.

Overshooting at the system level often throws the subsystem suppliers back to a stage where their product is not good enough for what the system assembler needs. Competitive forces consequently compel the subsystem suppliers to create architectures that are increasingly interdependent and proprietary as they try to push the bleeding edge of performance. They have to do this to win the business of their immediate customers, who are the designers and manufacturers of modular products. Hence, as a natural and inescapable result of the shift in industry structure, the place where companies are used to making a lot of money–the end-user stage–becomes unlikely to be the place where money will be made in the future. And, conversely, the places where attractive profits were rarely made in the past—components and subsystems—often become highly profitable.

The exhibit "Where the money went in the PC industry" illustrates how this worked in the desktop computer market in the 1990s. Initially, money flowed from the customer to the companies that designed and assembled computers; but as the decade progressed, less and less of it stopped there as profit. Quite a bit of this money flowed over to operating system maker Microsoft and lodged there. Another chunk flowed to processor manufacturer Intel and stopped there. Money flowed to the DRAM chip makers such as Samsung and Micron Technology as well, but not much of it stopped there. It flowed through them and accumulated instead at companies like

Where the money went in the PC industry

As PCs became good enough for mainstream users, profits flowed from the customers through the assemblers (the IBMs and Compaqs of the world) to lodge in the component makers—the operating system maker (Microsoft), the processor maker (Intel), and initially to the memory chip makers and disk drive manufacturers. But as DRAM chips and drives became good enough for the assemblers, the money flowed even further up the value chain to DRAM equipment makers and head and disk suppliers.

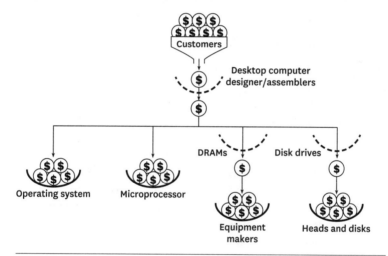

Applied Materials, which supplied the chip-manufacturing equipment that the DRAM makers used. Similarly, money flowed right through the assemblers of disk drives such as Quantum and lodged at the stage where heads and disks were made.

What's different about the places where the money collected and those where it didn't? For most of this period, profits lodged with the products that were the ones not yet good enough for what their immediate customers needed. The architectures of those products therefore tended to be interdependent and proprietary. Companies in the blue boxes could only hang onto subsistence profits because the functionality of their products tended to be more than good enough, and so their architectures had become modular.

Consider the DRAM industry. Because the architecture of their chips was modular, DRAM makers could not be satisfied with even the very best manufacturing equipment available. To succeed, DRAM producers needed to make their products at ever higher yields and ever lower costs. This rendered the functionality of the equipment that Applied Materials and other such companies made not good enough. As a consequence, the architecture of this equipment became interdependent and proprietary, as the equipment makers strove to inch closer to the performance their customers needed.

Where Companies Go Wrong

Once an industry starts to fragment, a very predictable thing happens to companies that design and assemble modular products. They face investor pressure to improve their return on assets but find that because they can't differentiate their products or make them at a lower cost than competitors, they can't improve the numerator of their ROA ratio. So they shrink the denominator; they sell off asset-intensive units that design and manufacture components to companies that see in those same operations the opportunity to create subsystems whose architectures are progressively more interdependent—thus improving the numerator of *their* ROA ratio. Lucent's recent spin-offs of its component and manufacturing operations is an example. This seems perfectly logical and necessary, given the increasingly modular character of many of Lucent's systems. But with perfect predictability, this pressure from Wall Street to boost ROA forces companies to skate away from the place where the money will be made in the future.

This scenario could soon play out in one of IBM's businesses. Through the 1990s, the capacity of the 2.5-inch disk drives used in notebook computers tended to be inadequate. True to form, their architectures were interdependent, and the design and assembly stage was very profitable. As the leading manufacturer, IBM enjoyed 40% gross margins. Now, drive capacity is becoming more than good enough for notebook computer makers, presaging the decline of what has been a beautiful business.

If IBM plays its cards right, however, it is actually in a very attractive position. As the most integrated drive maker, it can skate to where the money will be by using the advent of modularity to detach its head and disk operations from its disk drive design-and-assembly business. If IBM begins to sell its components aggressively to competing disk drive makers, it can continue to enjoy the most attractive profit levels in the industry. There was a time IBM could fight this particular war and win. Now, a better strategy is to sell bullets to the combatants.

IBM has already made similar moves in its computer business through its decisions to chop up its integrated value chain and aggressively sell its technology, components, and subsystems in the open market. Simultaneously, it has created a consulting and systems integration business at the high end and de-emphasized the design and assembly of computers. As IBM has skated to those points in the value chain where complex, nonstandard integration needed to occur, that has led to a remarkable—and remarkably profitable—transformation of a huge company. To the extent that an integrated company like IBM can flexibly couple and decouple its operations, rather than irrevocably sell off operations, it has greater potential than a nonintegrated company to thrive from one cycle to the next.

Where Will the Money Be in the Auto Industry?

We believe this model can help managers, strategists, and investors in a wide variety of industries see into the future with greater clarity than the traditional tools of historical data analysis have allowed. When we consider, for example, where the money in the automobile industry will go in the future, the car companies seem to be falling into exactly the same trap that IBM did some 15 years ago.

While automobiles often used to rust or fall apart mechanically well before their owners were ready to part with them, auto quality now has overshot what most customers want or need. In fact, the most reliable cars usually go out of style long before they wear out. As a result, the basis of competition is changing. Whereas it used to take six years to design a new car model, today it takes less than two. Car companies routinely compete by customizing features to the whims of smaller and smaller market niches. In the 1960s, it was not unusual for a model to sell a million units a year. Today, the market is far more fragmented: If you sell 200,000 units of a particular model, you're doing fine. Some makers now promise that you can walk into a dealership, custom order a car exactly to your desired configuration, and have it delivered in five days—roughly the response time that Dell Computer offers.

To compete in this way, automakers are adopting modular architectures for their mainstream models. Rather than knitting together individual components from diverse suppliers, they're procuring subsystems from fewer tier-one suppliers. The architecture within each subsystem—braking, steering, chassis, and the like—is becoming progressively more interdependent as these suppliers work to meet the auto assemblers' performance and cost demands. Inevitably, the subsystems' external interfaces are becoming more modular because the economics of using the same subsystem in several car models more than compensates for any compromises in performance that might result.

As the basis of competition has shifted, the vertically integrated automakers have had to break up their value chains so they can more quickly and flexibly incorporate the best components from the best suppliers. GM subsequently spun out its component operations into a separate company, Delphi Automotive Systems, and Ford has spun out its component operations as Visteon. Thus, the same thing is happening to the auto industry that happened to computers: Overshooting has precipitated a change in the basis of competition, which has precipitated a change in architecture, which has forced the dominant, integrated firms to dis-integrate.

To become fast and flexible, IBM's PC business outsourced its microprocessor to Intel and its operating system to Microsoft. But in the process, IBM hung onto where the money *had* been—the design and assembly of the computer system—and put into business the two companies that were positioned where the money *would* be. GM and Ford, with the encouragement of their investment bankers, have just done exactly the same thing. They have spun out the pieces of the value chain where the money will be in order to stay where the money has been.

Ford and GM had no choice but to decouple their component operations from their design-and-assembly businesses. Indeed, they gave their shareholders the option of owning one or both. But rather than an irreversible divestiture, they might have taken a page from IBM's recent forays into opportunistic decoupling, ignored the siren song of investment bankers, and found a way not to shed those asset- and scale-intensive businesses where the numerator of the ROA ratio will likely be more attractive in the future. This will be especially true if shifts in customer demand mandate some sort of reintegration in the future.

Managers of the slimmed-down automakers can still do well, but they'll need to dramatically change the way they do business in the design-and-assembly stage. They need to do in their industry what Dell did in the computer industry—become consummately fast, flexible, and convenient. Overshooting changes the game. If GM and Ford can play this new game better than competitors, they can still prosper, much as Dell did in the 1990s against competitors who hadn't mastered the new rules as effectively.

The implications of these findings are clear. The power to capture attractive profits will shift in the value chain *to* those activities where the immediate customer is not yet satisfied with the functionality of available products. It is in these stages that complex, interdependent integration occurs—activities that create steeper economies of scale and greater opportunities for differentiation. The power will shift *away* from activities where the immediate customer is more than satisfied because it is there that standard, modular integration occurs. In most markets, this power shift occurs tier by tier in a way that is quite predictable.

Executives whose companies are currently making lots of money ought not to wonder *whether* the power to earn attractive profits will shift, but *when*. If they watch for the signals, quite possibly they can prosper in all cycles, rather than in only one.

Originally published in November 2001. Reprint 0110D

Surviving Disruption

by Maxwell Wessel and Clayton M. Christensen

DISRUPTIVE INNOVATIONS are like missiles launched at your business. For 20 years we've described missile after missile that took aim and annihilated its target: Napster, Amazon, and the Apple Store devastated Tower Records and Musicland; tiny, underpowered personal computers grew to replace minicomputers and mainframes; digital photography made film practically obsolete.

And all along we've prescribed a single response to ensure that when the dust settles, you'll still have a viable business: Develop a disruption of your own before it's too late to reap the rewards of participation in new, high-growth markets—as Procter & Gamble did with Swiffer, Dow Corning with Xiameter, and Apple with the iPod, iTunes, the iPad, and (most spectacularly) the iPhone. That prescription is, if anything, even more imperative in an increasingly volatile world.

But it is also incomplete.

Disruption is less a single event than a process that plays out over time, sometimes quickly and completely, but other times slowly and incompletely. More than a century after the invention of air transport, cargo ships still crisscross the globe. More than 40 years after Southwest Airlines went public, tens of thousands of passengers fly daily with legacy carriers. A generation after the introduction of the VCR, box-office receipts are still an enormous component of film revenues. Managers must not only disrupt themselves but also consider the fate of their legacy operations, for which decades or more of profitability may lie ahead.

We propose a systematic way to chart the path and pace of disruption so that you can fashion a more complete strategic response. To determine whether a missile will hit you dead-on, graze you, or pass you altogether, you need to:

- Identify the strengths of your disrupter's business model;

- Identify your own relative advantages;

- Evaluate the conditions that would help or hinder the disrupter from co-opting your current advantages in the future.

To guide you in determining a disrupter's strengths, we introduce the concept of the *extendable core*—the aspect of its business model that allows the disrupter to maintain its performance advantage as

LEGACY BUSINESS **Handheld GPS**	DISRUPTER **Cell Phone GPS**	DISRUPTER ADVANTAGES
WHAT JOBS DO CUSTOMERS WANT THIS PRODUCT TO PERFORM?		GPS apps are included in the smartphone price GPS data are easily integrated with information from other apps, such as restaurant reviews and reservation systems
"Inform me about my surroundings" / "Get me to the meeting on time" / "Get me home safely"		**DISRUPTER DISADVANTAGES** Phones are fragile
In case of emergency, people still value the reliability of a rugged, waterproof GPS device with a long battery life, so creating durable devices with even longer-lasting batteries may help secure this niche. But disrupters may overcome new-technology barriers to making those improvements. **EASY TO DISRUPT**		Phones must be small enough to fit into a pocket, restricting their size and weight Batteries must be recharged more frequently because the phones are used for other tasks

Idea in Brief

Not all disruptive missiles are destined to hit you directly or right away. Disruptions that will not greatly affect you for years require you to consider the right path forward for your core business.

To do so, you need to identify (1) the disrupter's advantage, (2) your own advantage, and (3) how easily the disrupter might co-opt your advantage in the future.

New insights into the mechanism of disruption reveal that the disrupter's advantage stems from its *extendable core*—its ability to maintain radically lower prices as it creeps upmarket in search of more customers. Your advantage stems from how well you do the jobs your customers want you to do. Your prospects for the future depend on adjusting your current business model to perform those jobs better and on how likely the disrupter is to overcome the fundamental barriers in its path.

it creeps upmarket in search of more and more customers. We then explore how a deep understanding of what jobs people want your company to do for them—and what jobs the disrupter could do better with its extendable core—will give you a clearer picture of your relative advantage. We go on to delineate the barriers a disrupter would need to overcome to undermine you in the future. This approach will enable you to see which parts of your current business are most vulnerable to disruption and—just as important—which parts you can defend.

Where Advantage Lies

What makes an innovation disruptive? As our colleague Michael Raynor suggested in his book *The Innovator's Manifesto* (2011), all disruptive innovations stem from technological or business model advantages that can scale as disruptive businesses move upmarket in search of more-demanding customers. These advantages are what enable the extendable core; they differentiate disruption from mere price competition.

To understand this important distinction, consider Raynor's example of simple price competition in the hotel industry: A Holiday Inn provides a bed for the night for less (and in less luxury) than does the Four Seasons down the street. For the economy hotel chain to appeal to Four Seasons customers, it would have to invest in internal improvements, prime real estate, and an expensive service staff. Doing so would force it to adopt the same cost structure as the Four Seasons, so it would have to charge its customers similarly.

By contrast, in a disruptive innovation, an upstart can maintain its advantage while it improves its performance. What made the PC a disruptive innovation rather than just a low-end minicomputer, for instance, was the radical cost advantage its manufacturers achieved when they assembled their machines using standardized components. As component makers steadily improved the price and performance of their offerings, PC makers could preserve (or increase) their cost advantage even as they increased the power, capacity, and utility of their machines. This option was unavailable to minicomputer makers, because their improvements were derived from ever more effective designs of costly custom systems.

Not all the advantages of a disrupter's extendable core are so overpowering; often they are offset by disadvantages. Take the current disruption of higher education. Online universities can enroll, educate, and grant degrees to far more students at much lower cost than traditional institutions of higher learning can, because e-learning technologies enable every faculty member to reach far more people than any single professor could address in even the largest university lecture hall. The initial quality of e-learning institutions left something to be desired, but—as the theory of disruption predicts—they have been improving the effectiveness of their programs while maintaining their cost and convenience advantages, thus attracting more students away from traditional alternatives.

But consider two groups of students these online universities have difficulty serving. One group is those who are looking to burnish their résumés by demonstrating that they are good enough to get into an exclusive college. The online universities' extendable core is not much use here because their advantage lies in serving ever greater numbers of students with the same material—hardly a demonstration of exclusivity.

The other group is students who value the social aspects of college: the growth opportunities in living away from home, the close community of peers, the storied sports teams. E-learning institutions can (and do) opt to offer both online and on-campus courses in order to attract the widest variety of students, but they can't bring their full disruptive advantage to bear here, because each added service forces them further toward the cost structure of traditional universities. Novel partnerships or technological innovations might eventually enable them to address this problem, but their extendable core in its current form falls short of satisfying these students.

Identifying a disrupter's extendable core tells you what kinds of customers the disrupter might attract and—just as important—what kinds it won't. How many customers of each kind do you have? To answer that question, you need to consider what people are really doing when they buy your products and services.

LEGACY BUSINESS **Auto Sales**	DISRUPTER **Car Sharing**	DISRUPTER ADVANTAGES
WHAT JOBS DO CUSTOMERS WANT THIS PRODUCT TO PERFORM?		More cost-effective than ownership for infrequent drivers
		No need for insurance
"Get my kids safely to school" / "Help me get where I need to go when I need to go there" / "Provide a mobile office"		Parking is included
		Users can drive a variety of makes and models
Drivers who work in their cars value the ability to store and optimally arrange papers, laptops, luggage, and other items. Moving them from car to car would be highly inconvenient and time-consuming, so car sharing is unlikely to overcome this business-model barrier any time soon. **HARD TO DISRUPT**		**DISRUPTER DISADVANTAGES** Less cost-effective than ownership for frequent and long-distance drivers Cars aren't always available when needed

Where Advantage Matters

Why do people long for certain products and services in some situations but not in others? Experts in disruption have a ready answer: to complete some job that crops up in their lives. A college student doesn't go shopping for floor cleaner, sponges, and a bucket for their own sake. Something—say, the impending arrival of his parents—makes it necessary for him to clean his room, so he seeks some product or service with which to do it. The floor cleaner, sponges, and bucket have no intrinsic value for him. It's their ability to keep him on good terms with his family that he cares about.

Successful entrepreneurs naturally look at opportunities in terms of the jobs they can do for customers. An innovator observing the plight of our student might realize that he doesn't care about keeping his room clean all the time, so he's not interested in stocking up on cleaning supplies. Because he doesn't clean often and may not be good at it, he's probably looking for something simple and foolproof. And he has probably waited to clean until just before his parents arrive (so that his room will stay neat), which means he needs to do the job quickly. An enterprising fellow student might see that as an opportunity to start a 30-minute emergency cleaning service on campus. A consumer goods company might consider bundling small amounts of appropriate cleaning supplies and making them conveniently available at university bookstores, nearby pharmacies, or even coffee shops.

Identifying what jobs people need done and how they could be done more easily, conveniently, or affordably is what enables a disrupter to imagine how to improve its product to appeal to more and more of your customers. If you can determine how effective or ineffective the disrupter is likely to be at doing the jobs you currently do, you can identify the most vulnerable segments of your core business—and your most sustainable advantages. When a disruptive business offers a significant advantage and no disadvantages in doing the same job you do, disruption will be swift and complete (think online music versus CDs). But when the advantages of a disrupter's extendable core are ill suited to doing that job and its disadvantages are considerable, disruption will be slower and incomplete. Thus, at the simplest level, cargo ships are still in use because they're still much better than planes at transporting heavy goods. Box-office receipts still represent a large portion of studio revenues in part because sizable groups of people (teenage boys, dating couples) go to the movies to get out of the house. Ivy League universities are still better positioned than online institutions to confer elite status on aspiring high school seniors.

When Advantage Persists

Could something happen to make cargo ships obsolete or to decrease the value of an elite education? To find out, we need to consider how easily a disrupter could overcome its disadvantages in the future— to ask, "What would have to change for my current advantages to evaporate?" To approach this question, we propose a systematic assessment of five kinds of barriers to disruption, arranged here from easiest to overcome to hardest.

1. The momentum barrier (customers are used to the status quo)

2. The tech-implementation barrier (which could be overcome using existing technology)

3. The ecosystem barrier (which would require a change in the business environment to overcome)

4. The new-technologies barrier (the technology needed to change the competitive landscape does not yet exist)

5. The business model barrier (the disrupter would have to adopt your cost structure)

The more difficult the barrier, or the more barriers a disrupter faces, the more likely it is that customers will remain with incumbents. Cargo ships, whose containers are designed to move seamlessly from quay to rail to truck to loading dock, benefit from an ecosystem barrier, which airlines might conceivably assault with an integrated system of their own. Far more formidable, of course, is the new-technologies barrier to developing cheap, renewable jet fuel, which would enable airlines to dramatically lower the cost of air shipping.

This approach may seem intuitive, but decades of training have taught executives to focus not on the value they provide for their customers but on proxies for it—high-level profit and revenue data. If an innovator is causing a company losses, it's deemed threatening. If not, it's often dismissed. And overestimating a threat can be as costly as ignoring it: Managers struggle to keep customers who are unlikely to be lost to disruption in the same way they would compete with traditional rivals—by dropping prices or offering comparable product features. This sort of response both fails to identify the intrinsic advantage of the disrupter and ignores advantages that the legacy business could viably defend.

To many, it may be clear why ships still carry cargo and why the disruption of the movie theater by DVDs is incomplete. However, that clarity is easier to achieve in retrospect than it was on the precipice of disruption. During the 1980s content producers were up in arms over the spread of home video distribution. Today those same studios are fighting frantically to limit the adoption of digital streaming—which, although it certainly represents an improvement over (and a direct threat to) DVDs, remains at a distinct disadvantage in doing many of the jobs that movie theaters still perform.

To demonstrate how our approach can be applied both in more-ambiguous cases and in a prescriptive fashion, let's turn to a disruption that's occurring right now.

The Disruption of Retail Grocery Stores

Over the past 15 years online retailing has devastated traditional brick-and-mortar retailers. The disruption began with the swift destruction of companies such as Tower Records and Hollywood Video and has taken its toll on high-margin retailers like Neiman Marcus and Saks Fifth Avenue. Retail continues to be a hotbed of entrepreneurship and innovation.

One of the last bastions against this disruptive wave is the grocery industry. Only about 1% of all groceries in the United States are bought from online retailers like Peapod, NetGrocer, and FreshDirect.

However, we can expect that with an incentive to innovate their way upmarket, e-grocers will become increasingly significant. The theory of disruption tells us that these entrants will speed their delivery times, increase their product selection, and add features we can hardly imagine today in pursuit of new customers and higher profit margins. Even now, Amazon is making more and more grocery staples available online and is experimenting with discounted prices for automatic replenishment services. And Walmart has constructed convenient urban pickup centers for items bought online.

Questions for the executives of Kroger, Safeway, Whole Foods, and the like are "How complete will the grocery industry's disruption become?" and "What role will traditional brick-and-mortar stores play in the grocery market of the future?"

Online Grocers' Extendable Core

We all intuitively grasp the advantages of online retailing. But for businesses attempting to predict the extent and impact of disruption, intuition isn't always enough. When Amazon first opened its virtual doors, most people saw only its most salient advantage—the deep price discounts it could offer by passing along the cost savings it gained from dispensing with physical retail outlets. A more careful analysis of its business model revealed that cash flow was an even greater advantage: Consumers gave Amazon their money before Amazon had to pay its suppliers for inventory. (This was so lucrative that it helped to fund much of Amazon's early development.) Conceivably, anything sold online, whether books or cornflakes, has a similar advantage. Online grocers can reduce their inventory by centralizing warehouses and can pay less for products than traditional grocery chains do by purchasing them on an even greater scale. They don't have to pay costly sales staff. And sometimes, through careful warehouse placement, they can avoid paying state sales taxes.

On the downside, though, online grocers have to ship their products to individual homes—far more destinations than any brick-and-mortar grocer need worry about. They must manage complex logistics chains to coordinate shipments of the various items that make up a grocery order, whereas supermarket shoppers merely

LEGACY BUSINESS **Railroads**	DISRUPTER **Cars, Trucks, and Planes**	DISRUPTER ADVANTAGES

WHAT JOBS DO CUSTOMERS WANT THIS SERVICE TO PERFORM?

"Help me get home for the holidays"	"Get my products to customers quickly"	"Help me operate my business efficiently"

Manufacturers value rail's far lower cost so much that they locate factories on a rail line. For many customers this business model advantage currently outweighs both the speed advantage of airplanes and the flexibility advantage of trucks. So standardized rail containers, which can be stacked and easily transferred to ships or trucks, create a powerful ecosystem barrier to disruption.

HARD TO DISRUPT

DISRUPTER ADVANTAGES

Roads connect far more places than rail lines do

Trucks can more easily deliver items from any factory to any destination on a road

Airplanes can move people and cargo much faster than rail can

Airplanes can move people and cargo overseas

DISRUPTER DISADVANTAGES

Higher variable costs

Higher labor costs

toss everything into a cart and wheel it to the front of the store. The lack of sales staff limits customer service for online grocers. And for consumers, the convenience of shopping from home comes at the expense of direct physical contact with the goods.

Which of these advantages and disadvantages do the managers at Kroger and Whole Foods need to focus on? To answer that question, they must discover just how shoppers are using their stores.

The Jobs Brick-and-Mortar Grocers Do

We find that the best way to identify the jobs a company does for its customers is through a combination of extensive surveys, interviews, focus groups, and in-person observations. Spend a day near a Kroger exit, and you'll see a few distinct patterns. In the morning and early afternoon, many customers spend a substantial amount of time in all the store's aisles loading up large grocery carts. Occasionally a customer zips in to buy one or two items and checks out in the express lane. Late in the afternoon, a handful of customers are still filling their carts with staples, but far more are picking up fresh vegetables, proteins, and the occasional baked good.

At the end of the day, if you had taken notes and interviewed a few customers about what they came to the store to accomplish (and what alternatives they use for the same purpose), you'd probably be ready to identify at least some of the jobs customers were hiring Kroger to complete. The people filling their carts were stocking up on products they knew in advance they would need—the weekly grocery pickup. The ones zipping in and out were after some emergency item they'd forgotten or something essential sold only by that market. The shoppers arriving during the afternoon rush were gathering ingredients for that night's dinner. These three jobs are by no means comprehensive, but they are big enough drivers of the customer population to shed light on the pace of grocery's disruption and on what the industry will look like in its wake.

You might assume that this sort of intention analysis is common, but it happens far less often than it should. Advances in data collection and analysis have made it possible to get ever more detailed information about who's buying, what they're buying, how often they're buying, and whom they're with when they're buying. Typically, consulting firms and internal strategy teams take reams of such data, crunch the numbers, and organize people into segments such as "frequent shoppers," "young parents," and "discount hunters." These labels appear to be aimed at uncovering intentions, but they essentially remain descriptions of types of people, and thus tell us little about behavior in certain circumstances. For instance, at the onset of a disruption, we might know that Kroger's most frequent shoppers were young mothers, but we wouldn't know what they were doing when they came into the store. The same woman might on one occasion walk methodically up and down the aisles, stocking up on the week's nonperishables, and on another might be dashing in to grab a forgotten item or two. She might also be returning practically every evening at 5:30 to buy the ingredients for that night's dinner. Or not. Without an understanding of what she's trying to accomplish each time she visits, it's impossible to identify what innovations might matter to her when she walks through the door.

Once you understand what jobs customers most commonly hire you to do, it becomes much easier to begin evaluating how important the advantages and disadvantages of a disrupter's extendable core are to your business. Take the job of providing emergency goods. Imagine that it's 8:45 PM and you've just realized that you're out of toothpaste. You immediately head to a store to ensure that you'll avoid the costly impact of gingivitis. You're not thinking about the advantages of shopping from home, the selection offered by nearly infinite shelf space, or the low price afforded by scale. You're focused on instant delivery. In deciding which store to visit, you find yourself comparing the traditional competitive advantages of physical retailers such as 7-Eleven, CVS, and the supermarket. The decision comes down to which of those stores is closest to you and whether you think it will have your favorite toothpaste (or at least an acceptable alternative) in stock. In this situation an online retailer's advantages are simply not relevant to you.

Consider the job of buying dinner, and you'll reach a similar conclusion about the relative advantages of brick-and-mortar markets over online retailing. Interviews with shoppers who are picking up dinner ingredients reveal that they typically don't decide what they're going to buy until they're at the store. Many use the store's selection to narrow down the possibilities—seeing what looks appealing helps them with the task of planning dinner day after day. They are likely to place a high value on obtaining the freshest ingredients. Because each tomato, steak, or bunch of grapes is different, they want to pick up and examine the perishable ingredients they're considering. Although FreshDirect and Peapod may guarantee freshness, these shoppers feel comforted by seeing the product in person. Only a compelling offer, such as Gilt Taste's gourmet products at steeply reduced prices, can substitute for their own judgment. Absent such a strong point of differentiation, customers turn to supermarkets, farmers' markets, and corner stores to get the job done. The convenience of online retail is simply not enough.

Just as we can envision the difficulties a disrupter would have in completing the emergency-item and dinner-shopping jobs, we can see how vulnerable the staples-shopping job is. Shoppers stocking up on branded nonperishables such as canned tuna, coffee, pancake mix, and spaghetti sauce know what they want and generally don't require it immediately. A sizable number of them already wait until they need a sufficient quantity to justify a trip to BJ's or Costco. Shopping on Amazon and waiting a few days for the items to be delivered is not so different. This is the job, our analysis suggests, that is most susceptible to disruption by online grocers. The early successes of Diapers.com and Soap.com in selling branded nonperishables traditionally provided by physical grocery stores is a harbinger of the coming shift.

The Barriers to Disruption

We can see disruption on the horizon, but how close is it? Returning to the five barriers—momentum, tech implementation, ecosystem, new technologies, business model—we can see that for online grocers to overcome their disadvantage in doing the job of providing emergency goods, they would have to engage in a costly infrastructure extension, either to build their own stores and adopt their traditional competitors' cost structures, or to send delivery trucks out at nowhere near optimum capacity. So for this job, disrupters are hitting the formidable business model barrier. Because either change would destroy their advantage, we can label this disadvantage significant and difficult to overcome.

A disrupter that is trying to do the job of stocking up on staples clearly encounters no business model barrier, no new-technology barrier, no genuine tech-implementation barrier, and a weakening momentum barrier. Still, one could argue that daily trips to the grocery store for dinner or emergency items might make the thought of shopping online for nonperishables seem duplicative. But this is true only as long as it makes sense to shop at traditional grocery stores.

What if farmers' markets continue to proliferate, or if a traditional competitor—say, Trader Joe's—chooses to invest in smaller-format urban grocery stores that feature fewer staples and more fresh goods? Then it may well become sensible for consumers to shop for nonperishables separately. Because we can envision that such an ecosystem shift will result naturally from entrepreneurs' pursuit of profit, we predict that disruption will arrive sooner rather than later.

The Path Forward

Online grocers constitute a viable and potent threat when it comes to the job of delivering products we know in advance that we need. Customers who hire traditional grocers to do that job already value the broad selection and lower prices that online grocers are poised to provide. Over time, as they get used to shopping online, they may also come to value free delivery and the savings on gasoline they achieve by eliminating errands. As more customers adopt the on-line format, it will become ever more difficult for brick-and-mortar grocers to compete here. Legacy grocers could establish discount programs, secure exclusive distribution, put bigger stores in more-convenient locations, institute or expand loyalty programs that offer savings on gas to retain shoppers who are looking to stock up. But ultimately those efforts will be futile. As online grocers grow in scale, they will be able to offer better discount programs, match loyalty programs, work to secure the same exclusive distribution. Wise brick-and-mortar grocers won't fight this disruption head-on. They will instead focus on developing innovations aimed at completing their still-defensible jobs—serving the emergency shopper and the harried soul who is trying to put dinner on the table.

To better serve those customers, traditional grocery retailers should focus on outcompeting convenience stores with lower prices and better quality (particularly of perishables) and out-competing farmers' markets—perhaps with greater selection or by enticing farmers to sell produce inside their stores. They should be thinking hard about their physical advantages—considering how store layouts might help or hinder the shopper who is trying to gather ingredients for dinner. They might mimic England's Marks & Spencer by offering high-end semiprepared meals to recapture some of the margin lost from shrinking sales of branded nonperishables. Some might even experiment with locating shelf space inside other conveniently located retail outlets: A branded Trader Joe's aisle inside CVS would allow both retailers to better serve customers. Knowing where you're likely to succeed and where you're not is the key to making critical resource allocation decisions—not in the service of ephemeral short-term margins but in the realistic pursuit of longer-term competitive advantage.

The missiles of disruption are aimed at your local Kroger, Whole Foods, and Safeway. Their leaders should expect increasing competition from online upstarts for the highly profitable branded items that currently fill so many supermarket aisles. They would do well to plan for a world in which those revenues are in some large part lost to them forever.

Accepting the existence of a new competitive paradigm is never easy. It often forces us to acknowledge an inevitable loss of business. It may require us to develop disruptions that cannibalize our existing businesses. Failing to come to terms with these realities does us no service.

But neither does prematurely convincing ourselves of the singular superiority of a competitor's disruptive advantages. After all, Kroger, Whole Foods, and Safeway still perform important functions for millions of people that no online grocer will be able to perform anytime soon. Before leaders engage in reckless price competition or squander resources and effort in the futile defense of lost causes, they owe it to their shareholders, employees, and customers to take stock of the entire situation and respond comprehensively—to meet disrupters with disruption of their own, but also to guide their legacy businesses toward as healthy a future as possible.

Originally published in December 2012. Reprint R1212C

What Is Disruptive Innovation?

Twenty Years After the Introduction of the Theory, We Revisit What It Does—and Doesn't—Explain.

by Clayton M. Christensen, Michael E. Raynor, and Rory McDonald

THE THEORY OF DISRUPTIVE INNOVATION, introduced in *Harvard Business Review* in 1995, has proved to be a powerful way of thinking about innovation-driven growth. Many leaders of small, entrepreneurial companies praise it as their guiding star; so do many executives at large, well-established organizations, including Intel, Southern New Hampshire University, and Salesforce.com.

Unfortunately, disruption theory is in danger of becoming a victim of its own success. Despite broad dissemination, the theory's core concepts have been widely misunderstood and its basic tenets frequently misapplied. Furthermore, essential refinements in the theory over the past 20 years appear to have been overshadowed by the popularity of the initial formulation. As a result, the theory is sometimes criticized for shortcomings that have already been addressed.

There's another troubling concern: In our experience, too many people who speak of "disruption" have not read a serious book or article on the subject. Too frequently, they use the term loosely to invoke the concept of innovation in support of whatever it is they wish to do. Many researchers, writers, and consultants use "disruptive innovation" to describe *any* situation in which an industry is shaken up and previously successful incumbents stumble. But that's much too broad a usage.

The problem with conflating a disruptive innovation with any breakthrough that changes an industry's competitive patterns is that different types of innovation require different strategic approaches. To put it another way, the lessons we've learned about succeeding as a disruptive innovator (or defending against a disruptive challenger) will not apply to every company in a shifting market. If we get sloppy with our labels or fail to integrate insights from subsequent research and experience into the original theory, then managers may end up using the wrong tools for their context, reducing their chances of success. Over time, the theory's usefulness will be undermined.

This article is part of an effort to capture the state of the art. We begin by exploring the basic tenets of disruptive innovation and examining whether they apply to Uber. Then we point out some common pitfalls in the theory's application, how these arise, and why correctly using the theory matters. We go on to trace major turning points in the evolution of our thinking and make the case that what we have learned allows us to more accurately predict which businesses will grow.

First, a quick recap of the idea: "Disruption" describes a process whereby a smaller company with fewer resources is able to successfully challenge established incumbent businesses. Specifically, as incumbents focus on improving their products and services for their most demanding (and usually most profitable) customers, they exceed the needs of some segments and ignore the needs of others. Entrants that prove disruptive begin by successfully targeting those overlooked segments, gaining a foothold by delivering more-suitable functionality—frequently at a lower price. Incumbents, chasing higher profitability in more-demanding segments, tend not to respond vigorously. Entrants then move upmarket, delivering the performance that incumbents' mainstream customers require, while preserving the advantages that drove their early success.

Idea in Brief

The Issue

The ideas summed up in the phrase "disruptive innovation" have become a powerful part of business thinking—but they're in danger of losing their usefulness because they've been misunderstood and misapplied.

The Response

The leading authorities on disruptive innovation revisit the central tenets of disruption theory, its development over the past 20 years, and its limitations.

The Bottom Line

Does it matter whether Uber, say, is a disruptive innovation or something else entirely? It does: We can't manage innovation effectively if we don't grasp its true nature.

When mainstream customers start adopting the entrants' offerings in volume, disruption has occurred. (See the exhibit "The Disruptive Technologies Model" in "Skate to Where the Money Will Be" earlier in this volume.)

Is Uber a Disruptive Innovation?

Let's consider Uber, the much-feted transportation company whose mobile application connects consumers who need rides with drivers who are willing to provide them. Founded in 2009, the company has enjoyed fantastic growth (it operates in hundreds of cities in 60 countries and is still expanding). It has reported tremendous financial success (the most recent funding round implies an enterprise value in the vicinity of $50 billion). And it has spawned a slew of imitators (other start-ups are trying to emulate its "market-making" business model). Uber is clearly transforming the taxi business in the United States. But is it *disrupting* the taxi business?

According to the theory, the answer is no. Uber's financial and strategic achievements do not qualify the company as genuinely disruptive—although the company is almost always described that way. Here are two reasons why the label doesn't fit.

Disruptive innovations originate in low-end or new-market footholds. Disruptive innovations are made possible because they get started in two types of markets that incumbents overlook. *Low-end*

The Ubiquitous "Disruptive Innovation"

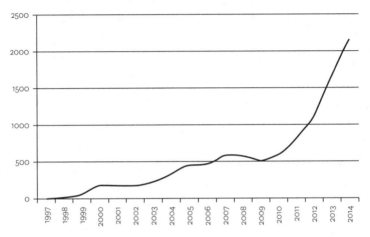

"Disruptive innovation" and "disruptive technology" are now part of the popular business lexicon, as suggested by the dramatic growth in the number of articles using those phrases in recent years.
Source: Factiva analysis of a wide variety of English–language publications.

footholds exist because incumbents typically try to provide their most profitable and demanding customers with ever-improving products and services, and they pay less attention to less-demanding customers. In fact, incumbents' offerings often overshoot the performance requirements of the latter. This opens the door to a disrupter focused (at first) on providing those low-end customers with a "good enough" product.

In the case of *new-market footholds,* disrupters create a market where none existed. Put simply, they find a way to turn nonconsumers into consumers. For example, in the early days of photocopying technology, Xerox targeted large corporations and charged high prices in order to provide the performance that those customers required. School librarians, bowling-league operators, and other small customers, priced out of the market, made do with carbon paper or mimeograph machines. Then in the late 1970s, new challengers introduced personal copiers, offering an affordable solution to individuals and small organizations—and a new market was created. From this relatively modest beginning, personal photocopier makers gradually built a major position in the mainstream photocopier market that Xerox valued.

A disruptive innovation, by definition, starts from one of those two footholds. But Uber did not originate in either one. It is difficult to claim that the company found a low-end opportunity: That would have meant taxi service providers had overshot the needs of a material number of customers by making cabs too plentiful, too easy to use, and too clean. Neither did Uber primarily target nonconsumers—people who found the existing alternatives so expensive or inconvenient that they took public transit or drove themselves instead: Uber was launched in San Francisco (a well-served taxi market), and Uber's customers were generally people already in the habit of hiring rides.

Uber has quite arguably been increasing total demand—that's what happens when you develop a better, less-expensive solution to a widespread customer need. But disrupters *start* by appealing to low-end or unserved consumers and then migrate to the mainstream market. Uber has gone in exactly the opposite direction: building a position in the mainstream market first and subsequently appealing to historically overlooked segments.

Disruptive innovations don't catch on with mainstream customers until quality catches up to their standards. Disruption theory differentiates disruptive innovations from what are called "sustaining innovations." The latter make good products better in the eyes of an incumbent's existing customers: the fifth blade in a razor, the clearer TV picture, better mobile phone reception. These improvements can be incremental advances or major breakthroughs, but they all enable firms to sell more products to their most profitable customers.

Disruptive innovations, on the other hand, are initially considered inferior by most of an incumbent's customers. Typically, customers are not willing to switch to the new offering merely because it is less expensive. Instead, they wait until its quality rises enough to satisfy them. Once that's happened, they adopt the new product and happily accept its lower price. (This is how disruption drives prices down in a market.)

Most of the elements of Uber's strategy seem to be sustaining innovations. Uber's service has rarely been described as inferior to existing taxis; in fact, many would say it is *better*. Booking a ride requires just a few taps on a smartphone; payment is cashless and convenient; and passengers can rate their rides afterward, which helps ensure high standards. Furthermore, Uber delivers service reliably and punctually, and its pricing is usually competitive with (or lower than) that of established taxi services. And as is typical when incumbents face threats from sustaining innovations, many of the taxi companies are motivated to respond. They are deploying competitive technologies, such as hailing apps, and contesting the legality of some of Uber's services.

Why Getting It Right Matters

Readers may still be wondering, Why does it matter what words we use to describe Uber? The company has certainly thrown the taxi industry into disarray: Isn't that "disruptive" enough? No. Applying the theory correctly is essential to realizing its benefits. For example, small competitors that nibble away at the periphery of your business very likely should be ignored—unless they are on a disruptive trajectory, in which case they are a potentially mortal threat. And both of these challenges are fundamentally different from efforts by competitors to woo your bread-and-butter customers.

As the example of Uber shows, identifying true disruptive innovation is tricky. Yet even executives with a good understanding of disruption theory tend to forget some of its subtler aspects when making strategic decisions. We've observed four important points that get overlooked or misunderstood:

1. **Disruption is a process.** The term "disruptive innovation" is misleading when it is used to refer to a product or service at one fixed point, rather than to the evolution of that product or service over time. The first minicomputers were disruptive not merely because

they were low-end upstarts when they appeared on the scene, nor because they were later heralded as superior to mainframes in many markets; they were disruptive by virtue of the path they followed from the fringe to the mainstream.

Most every innovation—disruptive or not—begins life as a small-scale experiment. Disrupters tend to focus on getting the business model, rather than merely the product, just right. When they succeed, their movement from the fringe (the low end of the market or a new market) to the mainstream erodes first the incumbents' market share and then their profitability. This process can take time, and incumbents can get quite creative in the defense of their established franchises. For example, more than 50 years after the first discount department store was opened, mainstream retail companies still operate their traditional department-store formats. Complete substitution, if it comes at all, may take decades, because the incremental profit from staying with the old model for one more year trumps proposals to write off the assets in one stroke.

The fact that disruption can take time helps to explain why incumbents frequently overlook disrupters. For example, when Netflix launched, in 1997, its initial service wasn't appealing to most of Blockbuster's customers, who rented movies (typically new releases) on impulse. Netflix had an exclusively online interface and a large inventory of movies, but delivery through the U.S. mail meant selections took five days to arrive. The service appealed to only a few customer groups—movie buffs who didn't care about new releases, early adopters of DVD players, and online shoppers. If Netflix had not eventually begun to serve a broader segment of the market, Blockbuster's decision to ignore this competitor would not have been a strategic blunder: The two companies filled very different needs for their (different) customers.

However, as new technologies allowed Netflix to shift to streaming video over the internet, the company did eventually become appealing to Blockbuster's core customers, offering a wider selection of content with an all-you-can-watch, on-demand, low-price, high-quality, highly convenient approach. And it got there via a classically disruptive path. If Netflix (like Uber) had begun by launching a service targeted at a larger competitor's core market, Blockbuster's response would very likely have been a vigorous and perhaps successful counterattack. But failing to respond effectively to the trajectory that Netflix was on led Blockbuster to collapse.

2. Disrupters often build business models that are very different from those of incumbents. Consider the health care industry. General practitioners operating out of their offices often rely on their years of experience and on test results to interpret patients' symptoms, make diagnoses, and prescribe treatment. We call this a "solution shop" business model. In contrast, a number of convenient care clinics are taking a disruptive path by using what we call a "process" business model: They follow standardized protocols to diagnose and treat a small but increasing number of disorders.

One high-profile example of using an innovative business model to effect a disruption is Apple's iPhone. The product that Apple debuted in 2007 was a sustaining innovation in the smartphone market: It targeted the same customers coveted by incumbents, and its initial success is likely explained by product superiority. The iPhone's subsequent growth is better explained by disruption—not of other smartphones but of the laptop as the primary access point to the internet. This was achieved not merely through product improvements but also through the introduction of a new business model. By building a facilitated network connecting application developers with phone users, Apple changed the game. The iPhone created a new market for internet access and eventually was able to challenge laptops as mainstream users' device of choice for going online.

3. Some disruptive innovations succeed; some don't. A third common mistake is to focus on the results achieved—to claim that a company is disruptive by virtue of its success. But success is not built into the definition of disruption: Not every disruptive path leads to a triumph, and not every triumphant newcomer follows a disruptive path.

For example, any number of internet-based retailers pursued disruptive paths in the late 1990s, but only a small number prospered. The failures are not evidence of the deficiencies of disruption theory; they are simply boundary markers for the theory's application. The theory says very little about how to win in the foothold market, other than to play the odds and avoid head-on competition with better-resourced incumbents.

If we call every business success a "disruption," then companies that rise to the top in very different ways will be seen as sources of insight into a common strategy for succeeding. This creates a danger: Managers may mix and match behaviors that are very likely inconsistent with one another and thus unlikely to yield the hoped-for result. For example, both Uber and Apple's iPhone owe their success to a platform-based model: Uber digitally connects riders with drivers; the iPhone connects app developers with phone users. But Uber, true to its nature as a sustaining innovation, has focused on expanding its network and functionality in ways that make it better than traditional taxis. Apple, on the other hand, has followed a disruptive path by building its ecosystem of app developers so as to make the iPhone more like a personal computer.

4. The mantra "Disrupt or be disrupted" can misguide us. Incumbent companies do need to respond to disruption if it's occurring, but they should not overreact by dismantling a still-profitable business. Instead, they should continue to strengthen relationships with core customers by investing in sustaining innovations. In addition, they can create a new division focused solely on the growth opportunities that arise from the disruption. Our research suggests that the success of this new enterprise depends in large part on keeping it separate from the core business. That means that for some time, incumbents will find themselves managing two very different operations.

Of course, as the stand-alone business grows, it may eventually steal customers from the core. But corporate leaders should not try to solve this problem before it *is* a problem.

What a Disruptive Innovation Lens Can Reveal

It is rare that a technology or product is inherently sustaining or disruptive. And when new technology is developed, disruption theory does not dictate what managers should do. Instead it helps them make a strategic choice between taking a sustaining path and taking a disruptive one.

The theory of disruption predicts that when an entrant tackles incumbent competitors head-on, offering better products or services, the incumbents will accelerate their innovations to defend their business. Either they will beat back the entrant by offering even better services or products at comparable prices, or one of them will acquire the entrant. The data supports the theory's prediction that entrants pursuing a sustaining strategy for a standalone business will face steep odds: In Christensen's seminal study of the disk drive industry, only 6% of sustaining entrants managed to succeed.

Uber's strong performance therefore warrants explanation. According to disruption theory, Uber is an outlier, and we do not have a universal way to account for such atypical outcomes. In Uber's case, we believe that the regulated nature of the taxi business is a large part of the answer. Market entry and prices are closely controlled in many jurisdictions. Consequently, taxi companies have rarely innovated. Individual drivers have few ways to innovate, except to defect to Uber. So Uber is in a unique situation relative to taxis: It can offer better quality and the competition will find it hard to respond, at least in the short term.

To this point, we've addressed only whether or not Uber is disruptive to the taxi business. The limousine or "black car" business is a different story, and here Uber is far more likely to be on a disruptive path. The company's UberSELECT option provides more-luxurious cars and is typically more expensive than its standard service—but typically less expensive than hiring a traditional limousine. This lower price imposes some compromises, as UberSELECT currently does not include one defining feature of the leading incumbents in this market: acceptance of advance reservations. Consequently, this offering from Uber appeals to the low end of the limousine service market: customers willing to sacrifice a measure of convenience for monetary savings. Should Uber find ways to match or exceed incumbents' performance levels without compromising its cost and price advantage, the company appears to be well positioned to move into the mainstream of the limo business—and it will have done so in classically disruptive fashion.

How Our Thinking About Disruption Has Developed

Initially, the theory of disruptive innovation was simply a statement about correlation. Empirical findings showed that incumbents outperformed entrants in a sustaining innovation context but underperformed in a disruptive innovation context. The reason for this correlation was not immediately evident, but one by one, the elements of the theory fell into place.

First, researchers realized that a company's propensity for strategic change is profoundly affected by the interests of customers who provide the resources the firm needs to survive. In other words, incumbents (sensibly) listen to their existing customers and concentrate on sustaining innovations as a result. Researchers then arrived at a second insight: Incumbents' focus on their existing customers becomes institutionalized in internal processes that make it difficult for even senior managers to shift investment to disruptive innovations. For example, interviews with managers of established companies in the disk drive industry revealed that resource allocation processes prioritized sustaining innovations (which had high margins and targeted large markets with well-known customers) while inadvertently starving disruptive innovations (meant for smaller markets with poorly defined customers).

Those two insights helped explain why incumbents rarely responded effectively (if at all) to disruptive innovations, but not why entrants eventually moved upmarket to challenge incumbents, over and over again. It turns out, however, that the same forces leading incumbents to ignore early-stage disruptions also compel disrupters ultimately to disrupt.

What we've realized is that, very often, low-end and new-market footholds are populated not by a lone would-be disrupter, but by several comparable entrant firms whose products are simpler, more convenient, or less costly than those sold by incumbents. The incumbents provide a de facto price umbrella, allowing many of the entrants to enjoy profitable growth within the foothold market. But that lasts only for a time: As incumbents (rationally, but mistakenly) cede the foothold market, they effectively remove the price umbrella, and price-based competition among the entrants reigns. Some entrants will founder, but the smart ones—the true disrupters—will improve their products and drive upmarket, where, once again, they can compete at the margin against higher-cost established competitors. The disruptive effect drives every competitor—incumbent and entrant—upmarket.

With those explanations in hand, the theory of disruptive innovation went beyond simple correlation to a theory of causation as well. The key elements of that theory have been tested and validated through studies of many industries, including retail, computers, printing, motorcycles, cars, semiconductors, cardiovascular surgery, management education, financial services, management consulting, cameras, communications, and computer-aided design software.

Making sense of anomalies. Additional refinements to the theory have been made to address certain anomalies, or unexpected scenarios, that the theory could not explain. For example, we originally assumed that any disruptive innovation took root in the lowest tiers of an established market—yet sometimes new entrants seemed to be competing in entirely new markets. This led to the distinction we discussed earlier between low-end and new-market footholds.

Low-end disrupters (think steel minimills and discount retailers) come in at the bottom of the market and take hold within an existing value network before moving upmarket and attacking that stratum (think integrated steel mills and traditional retailers). By contrast, new-market disruptions take hold in a completely new value network and appeal to customers who have previously gone without the product. Consider the transistor pocket radio and the PC: They were largely ignored by manufacturers of tabletop radios and mini-computers, respectively, because they were aimed at nonconsumers of those goods. By postulating that there are two flavors of foothold markets in which disruptive innovation can begin, the theory has become more powerful and practicable.

Another intriguing anomaly was the identification of industries that have resisted the forces of disruption, at least until very recently. Higher education in the United States is one of these. Over the years—indeed, over more than 100 years—new kinds of institutions with different initial charters have been created to address the needs of various population segments, including nonconsumers. Land-grant universities, teachers' colleges, two-year colleges, and so on were initially launched to serve those for whom a traditional four-year liberal arts education was out of reach or unnecessary.

Many of these new entrants strived to improve over time, compelled by analogues of the pursuit of profitability: a desire for growth, prestige, and the capacity to do greater good. Thus they made costly investments in research, dormitories, athletic facilities, faculty, and so on, seeking to emulate more-elite institutions. Doing so has increased their level of performance in some ways—they can provide richer learning and living environments for students, for example. Yet the *relative* standing of higher-education institutions remains largely unchanged: With few exceptions, the top 20 are still the top 20, and the next 50 are still in that second tier, decade after decade.

Because both incumbents and newcomers are seemingly following the same game plan, it is perhaps no surprise that incumbents are able to maintain their positions. What has been missing—until recently—is experimentation with new models that successfully appeal to today's nonconsumers of higher education.

The question now is whether there is a novel technology or business model that allows new entrants to move upmarket without emulating the incumbents' high costs—that is, to follow a disruptive path. The answer seems to be yes, and the enabling innovation is online learning, which is becoming broadly available. Real tuition for online courses is falling, and accessibility and quality are improving. Innovators are making inroads into the mainstream market at a stunning pace.

Will online education disrupt the incumbents' model? And if so, when? In other words, will online education's trajectory of improvement intersect with the needs of the mainstream market?

We've come to realize that the steepness of any disruptive trajectory is a function of how quickly the enabling technology improves. In the steel industry, continuous-casting technology improved quite slowly, and it took more than 40 years before the minimill Nucor matched the revenue of the largest integrated steelmakers. In contrast, the digital technologies that allowed personal computers to disrupt minicomputers improved much more quickly; Compaq was able to increase revenue more than tenfold and reach parity with the industry leader, DEC, in only 12 years.

Understanding what drives the rate of disruption is helpful for predicting outcomes, but it doesn't alter the way disruptions should be managed. Rapid disruptions are not fundamentally different from any others; they don't have different causal mechanisms and don't require conceptually different responses.

Similarly, it is a mistake to assume that the strategies adopted by some high-profile entrants constitute a special kind of disruption. Often these are simply miscategorized. Tesla Motors is a current and salient example. One might be tempted to say the company is disruptive. But its foothold is in the high end of the auto market (with customers willing to spend $70,000 or more on a car), and this segment is not uninteresting to incumbents. Tesla's entry, not surprisingly, has elicited significant attention and investment from established competitors. If disruption theory is correct, Tesla's future holds either acquisition by a much larger incumbent or a years-long and hard-fought battle for market significance.

We still have a lot to learn. We are eager to keep expanding and refining the theory of disruptive innovation, and much work lies ahead. For example, universally effective responses to disruptive threats remain elusive. Our current belief is that companies should create a separate division that operates under the protection of senior leadership to explore and exploit a new disruptive model. Sometimes this works—and sometimes it doesn't. In certain cases, a failed response to a disruptive threat cannot be attributed to a lack of understanding, insufficient executive attention, or inadequate financial investment. The challenges that arise from being an incumbent and an entrant simultaneously have yet to be fully specified; how best to meet those challenges is still to be discovered.

Disruption theory does not, and never will, explain everything about innovation specifically or business success generally. Far too many other forces are in play, each of which will reward further study. Integrating them all into a comprehensive theory of business success is an ambitious goal, one we are unlikely to attain anytime soon.

But there is cause for hope: Empirical tests show that using disruptive theory makes us measurably and significantly more accurate in our predictions of which fledgling businesses will succeed. As an ever-growing community of researchers and practitioners continues to build on disruption theory and integrate it with other perspectives, we will come to an even better understanding of what helps firms innovate successfully.

Originally published in December 2015. Reprint R1512B

Why Hard-Nosed Executives Should Care About Management Theory

by Clayton M. Christensen and Michael E. Raynor

IMAGINE GOING to your doctor because you're not feeling well. Before you've had a chance to describe your symptoms, the doctor writes out a prescription and says, "Take two of these three times a day, and call me next week."

"But—I haven't told you what's wrong," you say. "How do I know this will help me?"

"Why wouldn't it?" says the doctor. "It worked for my last two patients."

No competent doctors would ever practice medicine like this, nor would any sane patient accept it if they did. Yet professors and consultants routinely prescribe such generic advice, and managers routinely accept such therapy, in the naive belief that if a particular course of action helped other companies to succeed, it ought to help theirs, too.

Consider telecommunications equipment provider Lucent Technologies. In the late 1990s, the company's three operating divisions were reorganized into 11 "hot businesses." The idea was that each business would be run largely independently, as if it were an internal entrepreneurial start-up. Senior executives proclaimed that this approach would vault the company to the next level of growth and profitability by pushing decision making down the hierarchy and closer to the marketplace, thereby enabling faster, better-focused innovation. Their belief was very much in fashion; decentralization and autonomy appeared to have helped other large companies. And the startups that seemed to be doing so well at the time were all small, autonomous, and close to their markets. Surely what was good for them would be good for Lucent.

It turned out that it wasn't. If anything, the reorganization seemed to make Lucent slower and less flexible in responding to its customers' needs. Rather than saving costs, it added a whole new layer of costs.

How could this happen? How could a formula that helped other companies become leaner, faster, and more responsive have caused the opposite at Lucent?

It happened because the management team of the day and those who advised it acted like the patient and the physician in our opening vignette. The remedy they used—forming small, product-focused, close-to-the-customer business units to make their company more innovative and flexible—actually does work, when business units are selling modular, self-contained products. Lucent's leading customers operated massive telephone networks. They were buying not plug-and-play products but, rather, complicated system solutions whose components had to be knit together in an intricate way to ensure that they worked correctly and reliably. Such systems are best designed, sold, and serviced by employees who are not hindered from coordinating their interdependent interactions by being separated into unconnected units. Lucent's managers used a theory that wasn't appropriate to their circumstance—with disastrous results.

Theory, you say? Theory often gets a bum rap among managers because it's associated with the word "theoretical," which connotes "impractical." But it shouldn't. A theory is a statement predicting which actions will lead to what results and why. Every action that

Idea in Brief

You've got a problem to solve. Perhaps a decline in profitability, a rise in workforce turnover, delays in product development. The management books, articles, and consultants' reports amassed in your office are brimming with conflicting suggestions: "Decentralize decision making in your company!" "Vertically integrate!" "Focus on your core competencies!" "Branch out!"

Each practice sounds promising—and comes with impressive stories about companies that successfully applied it. But how do you sift through the contradictions? And what about that time you tried applying an intriguing new practice—with disastrous results? Which management theories should you *trust*?

The problem is that a theory that helps one company succeed can be fatal for another operating under different conditions. When Lucent, for example, followed advice to decentralize into independent "hot

businesses" in an effort to become leaner, faster, and more responsive, disaster ensued: Costs soared, service faltered, and customers complained. Why? Decentralization can make some companies more flexible—if business units are selling modular, self-contained products, for example. Lucent's customers, however, operated massive telephone networks and required complex system solutions with interdependent components. Under these conditions, decentralization only made it more difficult for employees to coordinate their interdependent activities to design, sell, and service the systems.

So how can you become a discerning consumer of managerial theory—selecting the practices most likely to help *your* company, given its unique circumstances? Understand what constitutes *sound* management theory. Then shrewdly evaluate the claims you encounter—no matter what their source.

managers take, and every plan they formulate, is based on some theory in the back of their minds that makes them expect the actions they contemplate will lead to the results they envision. But just like Monsieur Jourdain in Molière's *Le Bourgeois Gentilhomme*, who didn't realize he had been speaking prose all his life, most managers don't realize that they are voracious users of theory.

Good theories are valuable in at least two ways. First, they help us make predictions. Gravity, for example, is a theory. As a statement of

Idea in Practice

How Theories Develop

Theories are statements predicting which actions will lead to what results—and why. Sound theories help us make predictions ("If we do X, then Y will happen") and interpret the present ("Here's what's happening now and why"). Researchers develop theories by refining hypotheses to predict with increasing accuracy how a phenomenon should work in a widening range of circumstances. Theories develop in three stages:

- **Observe and describe a phenomenon**—for example, diversification strategies that succeed. At this early stage, researchers risk laying a foundation for unsound theories by simply observing a few successful companies, identifying some practices that they have in common, and concluding that these practices will work at *all* companies.

- **Classify aspects of the phenomenon into categories**—for instance, vertical versus horizontal diversification strategies. This process highlights meaningful differences among complex phenomena.

- **Formulate a hypothesis of what causes the phenomenon, and why.**

What Theories Do

Sound theories accomplish the following:

- **Pinpoint causation.** Correlation and causation aren't the same. For example, just because some successful companies have used venture capital funding doesn't mean such funding caused their success. It may have. But until we know what it is about venture capital that contributes to firms' success, we haven't pinpointed the *causal mechanism*. Venture funding remains merely an attribute or characteristic. We don't yet have a theory.

- **Move toward predictability.** Theories enable predictability

cause and effect, it allows us to predict that if we step off a cliff we will fall, without requiring that we actually try it to see what happens. Indeed, because reliable data are available solely about the past, using solid theories of causality is the only way managers can look into the future with any degree of confidence. Second, sound theories help us interpret the present, to understand what is happening and why. Theories help us sort the signals that portend important changes in the future from the noise that has no strategic meaning.

when they identify the causes behind results *and* the circumstances in which that causal mechanism will—and won't—result in success.

- **Analyze failures.** When companies do exactly what a theory prescribes but don't get the expected results, these "failures" become valuable opportunities for researchers to further hone their theories—by analyzing the phenomenon more closely and fine-tuning the theory. Failures help researchers avoid making one-size-fits-all recommendations.

Become a Discerning Consumer of Theory

How to avoid buying into unsound theories? Consider these guidelines:

- Beware of articles and books urging revolutionary change of everything. No single finding applies to all companies in all situations. You need to know not only where, when, and why

things should change, but also what should stay the same.

- Watch for research that classifies phenomena into categories based solely on attributes or characteristics. Such studies represent only a preliminary step toward reliable theories.

- Look for adjectives in correlation statements masquerading as causation. For example, "*Venture-capital* funding helps start-ups succeed." Sound theories describe *how* something works.

  Venture capitalists mete out small amounts of funds for many experiments. That encourages start-ups to abandon unsuccessful initiatives immediately and try new approaches—boosting their chances of success.

- Rarely consider positive research findings the final word. Progress comes when researchers refine a theory to explain situations in which the theory previously *failed*.

Establishing the central role that theory plays in managerial decision making is the first of three related objectives we hope to accomplish in this article. We will also describe how good theories are developed and give an idea of how a theory can improve over time. And, finally, we'd like to help managers develop a sense, when they read an article or a book, for what theories they can and cannot trust. Our overarching goal is to help managers become intelligent consumers of managerial theory so that the best work coming out of universities and consulting firms is put to good use—and the less thoughtful, less rigorous work doesn't do too much harm.

Where Theory Comes From

The construction of a solid theory proceeds in three stages. It begins with a description of some phenomenon we wish to understand. In physics, the phenomenon might be the behavior of high-energy particles; in business, it might be innovations that succeed or fail in the marketplace. In the exhibit, this stage is depicted as a broad foundation. That's because unless the phenomenon is carefully observed and described in its breadth and complexity, good theory cannot be built. Researchers surely head down the road to bad theory when they impatiently observe a few successful companies, identify some practices or characteristics that these companies seem to have in common, and then conclude that they have seen enough to write an article or book about how all companies can succeed. Such articles might suggest the following arguments, for example:

- Because Europe's wireless telephone industry was so successful after it organized around a single GSM standard, the wireless industry in the United States would have seen higher usage rates sooner if it, too, had agreed on a standard before it got going.

- If you adopt this set of best practices for partnering with best-of-breed suppliers, your company will succeed as these companies did.

Such studies are dangerous exactly because they would have us believe that because a certain medicine has helped some companies, it will help all companies. To improve understanding beyond this stage, researchers need to move to the second step: classifying aspects of the phenomenon into categories. Medical researchers sort diabetes into adult onset versus juvenile onset, for example. And management researchers sort diversification strategies into vertical versus horizontal types. This sorting allows researchers to organize complex and confusing phenomena in ways that highlight their most meaningful differences. It is then possible to tackle stage three, which is to formulate a hypothesis of what causes the phenomenon to happen and why. And that's a theory.

How do researchers improve this preliminary theory, or hypothesis? As the downward loop in the diagram below suggests, the process is iterative. Researchers use their theory to predict what they will see when they observe further examples of the phenomenon in the various categories they had defined in the second step. If the theory accurately predicts what they are observing, they can use it with increasing confidence to make predictions in similar circumstances.[1]

In their further observations, however, researchers often see something the theory cannot explain or predict, an anomaly that suggests something else is going on. They must then cycle back to the categorization stage and add or eliminate categories—or, sometimes, rethink them entirely. The researchers then build an improved theory upon the new categorization scheme. This new theory still explains the previous observations, but it also explains those that had seemed anomalous. In other words, the theory can now predict more accurately how the phenomenon should work in a wider range of circumstances.

To see how a theory has improved, let's look at the way our understanding of international trade has evolved. It was long thought

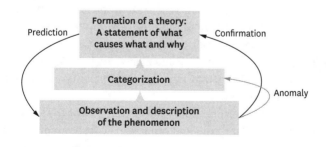

that countries with cheap, abundant resources would have an advantage competing in industries in which such resources are used as important inputs of production. Nations with inexpensive electric power, for example, would have a comparative advantage in making products that require energy-intensive production methods. Those with cheap labor would excel in labor-intensive products, and so on. This theory prevailed until Michael Porter saw anomalies the theory could not account for. Japan, with no iron ore and little coal, became a successful steel producer. Italy became the world's dominant producer of ceramic tile, even though its electricity costs were high and it had to import much of the clay.

Porter's theory of competitive clusters grew out of his efforts to account for these anomalies. Clusters, he postulated, lead to intense competition, which leads companies to optimize R&D, production, training, and logistics processes. His insights did not mean that prior notions of advantages based on low-cost resources were wrong, merely that they didn't adequately predict the outcome in every situation. So, for example, Canada's large pulp and paper industry can be explained in terms of relatively plentiful trees, and Bangalore's success in computer programming can be explained in terms of plentiful, low-cost, educated labor. But the competitive advantage that certain industries in Japan, Italy, and similar places have achieved can be explained only in terms of industry clusters. Porter's refined theory suggests that in one set of circumstances, where some otherwise scarce and valuable resource is relatively abundant, a country can and should exploit this advantage and so prosper. In another set of circumstances, where such resources are not available, policy makers can encourage the development of clusters to build process-based competitive advantages. Governments of nations like Singapore and Ireland have used Porter's theory to devise cluster-building policies that have led to prosperity in just the way his refined theory predicts.

We'll now take a closer look at three aspects of the theory-building process: the importance of explaining what causes an outcome (instead of just describing attributes empirically associated with that outcome); the process of categorization that enables theorists to move from tentative understanding to reliable predictions; and the importance of studying failures to building good theory.

Pinpointing Causation

In the early stages of theory building, people typically identify the most visible attributes of the phenomenon in question that appear to be *correlated* with a particular outcome and use those attributes as the basis for categorization. This is necessarily the starting point of theory building, but it is rarely ever more than an important first step. It takes a while to develop categories that capture a deep understanding of what *causes* the outcome.

Consider the history of people's attempts to fly. Early researchers observed strong correlations between being able to fly and having feathers and wings. But when humans attempted to follow the "best practices" of the most successful flyers by strapping feathered wings onto their arms, jumping off cliffs, and flapping hard, they were not successful because, as strong as the correlations were, the would-be aviators had not understood the fundamental causal mechanism of flight. When these researchers categorized the world in terms of the most obvious visible attributes of the phenomenon (wings versus no wings, feathers versus no feathers, for example), the best they could do was a statement of *correlation*—that the possession of those attributes is associated with the ability to fly.

Researchers at this stage can at best express their findings in terms of degrees of uncertainty: "Because such a large percentage of those with wings and feathers can fly when they flap (although ostriches, emus, chickens, and kiwis cannot), in all probability I will be able to fly if I fabricate wings with feathers glued on them, strap them to my arms, and flap hard as I jump off this cliff." Those who use research still in this stage as a guide to action often get into trouble because they confuse the correlation between attributes and outcomes with the underlying causal mechanism. Hence, they do what they think is necessary to succeed, but they fail.

A stunning number of articles and books about management similarly confuse the correlation of attributes and outcomes with causality. Ask yourself, for example, if you've ever seen studies that:

- contrast the success of companies funded by venture capital with those funded by corporate capital (implying that the source of capital funding is a cause of success rather than merely an attribute that can be associated with a company that happens to be successful for some currently unknown reason).

- contend that companies run by CEOs who are plain, ordinary people earn returns to shareholders that are superior to those of companies run by flashy CEOs (implying that certain CEO personality attributes cause company performance to improve).

- assert that companies that have diversified beyond those SIC codes that define their core businesses return less to their shareholders than firms that kept close to their core (thus leaping to the conclusion that the attributes of diversification or centralization cause shareholder value creation).

- conclude that 78% of female home owners between the ages of 25 and 35 prefer this product over that one (thus implying that the attributes of home ownership, age, and gender somehow cause people to prefer a specific product).

None of these studies articulates a theory of causation. All of them express a correlation between attributes and outcomes, and that's generally the best you can do when you don't understand what causes a given outcome. In the first case, for example, studies have shown that 20% of start-ups funded by venture capitalists succeed, another 50% end up among the walking wounded, and the rest fail altogether. Other studies have shown that the success rate of start-ups funded by corporate capital is much, much lower. But from such studies you can't conclude that your start-up will succeed if it is funded by venture capital. You must first know what it is about venture capital—the mechanism—that contributes to a start-up's success.

In management research, unfortunately, many academics and consultants intentionally remain at this correlation-based stage of theory building in the mistaken belief that they can increase the predictive power of their "theories" by crunching huge databases on powerful computers, producing regression analyses that measure the correlations of attributes and outcomes with ever higher degrees of statistical significance. Managers who attempt to be guided by such research can only hope that they'll be lucky—that if they acquire the recommended attributes (which on average are associated with success), somehow they too will find themselves similarly blessed with success.

The breakthroughs that lead from categorization to an understanding of fundamental causality generally come not from crunching ever more data but from highly detailed field research, when researchers crawl inside companies to observe carefully the causal processes at work. Consider the progress of our understanding of Toyota's production methods. Initially, observers noticed that the strides Japanese companies were making in manufacturing outpaced those of their counterparts in the United States. The first categorization efforts were directed vaguely toward the most obvious attribute—that perhaps there was something in Japanese culture that made the difference.

When early researchers visited Toyota plants in Japan to see its production methods (often called "lean manufacturing"), though, they observed more significant attributes of the system—inventories that were kept to a minimum, a plant-scheduling system driven by kanban cards instead of computers, and so on. But unfortunately, they leaped quickly from attributes to conclusions, writing books assuring managers that if they, too, built manufacturing systems with these attributes, they would achieve improvements in cost, quality, and speed comparable to those Toyota enjoys. Many manufacturers tried to make their plants conform to these lean attributes—and while many reaped some improvements, none came close to replicating what Toyota had done.

The research of Steven Spear and Kent Bowen has advanced theory in this field from such correlations by suggesting fundamental causes of Toyota's ability to continually improve quality, speed, and cost. Spear went to work on several Toyota assembly lines for some time. He began to see a pattern in the way people thought when they designed any process—those for training workers, for instance, or installing car seats, or maintaining equipment. From this careful and extensive observation, Spear and Bowen concluded that all processes at Toyota are designed according to four specific rules that create automatic feedback loops, which repeatedly test the effectiveness of each new activity, pointing the way toward continual improvements. (For a detailed account of Spear and Bowen's theory, see "Decoding the DNA of the Toyota Production System," HBR September–October 1999.) Using this mechanism, organizations as diverse as hospitals, aluminum smelters, and semiconductor fabricators have begun achieving improvements on a scale similar to Toyota's, even though their processes often share few visible attributes with Toyota's system.

Moving Toward Predictability

Manned flight began to be *possible* when Daniel Bernoulli's study of fluid mechanics helped him understand the mechanism that creates lift. Even then, though, understanding the mechanism itself wasn't enough to make manned flight perfectly *predictable*. Further research was needed to identify the circumstances under which that mechanism did and did not work.

When aviators used Bernoulli's understanding to build aircraft with airfoil wings, some of them still crashed. They then had to figure out what it was about those circumstances that led to failure. They, in essence, stopped asking the question, "What attributes are associated with success?" and focused on the question, "Under what circumstances will the use of this theory lead to failure?" They learned, for example, that if they climbed too steeply, insufficient lift was created. Also, in certain types of turbulence, pockets of relatively lower-density air forming under a wing could cause a sudden down spin. As aviators came to recognize those circumstances that required different technologies and piloting techniques and others that made attempting flight too dangerous, manned flight became not just possible but predictable.

In management research, similar breakthroughs in predictability occur when researchers not only identify the causal mechanism that ties actions to results but go on to describe the circumstances in which that mechanism does and does not result in success. This enables them to discover whether and how managers should adjust the way they manage their organizations in these different circumstances. Good theories, in other words, are *circumstance contingent*: They define not just what causes what and why, but also how the causal mechanism will produce different outcomes in different situations.

For example, two pairs of researchers have independently been studying why it is so difficult for companies to deliver superior returns to shareholders over a sustained period. They have recently published carefully researched books on the question that reach opposing conclusions. *Profit from the Core* observes that the firms whose performance is best and lasts longest are, on average, those that have sought growth in areas close to the skills they'd honed in their core businesses. It recommends that other managers follow suit. *Creative Destruction,* in contrast, concludes that because most attractive businesses ultimately lose their luster, managers need to bring the dynamic workings of entrepreneurial capitalism inside their companies and be willing to create new core businesses.

Because they've juxtaposed their work in such a helpful way, we can see that what the researchers actually have done is define the critical question that will lead to the predictability stage of the theory-building cycle: "Under what circumstances will staying close to the core help me sustain superior returns, and when will it be critical to set the forces of creative destruction to work?" When the researchers have defined the set of different situations in which managers might find themselves relative to this question and then articulated a circumstance-contingent theory, individuals can begin following their recommendations with greater confidence that they will be on the right path for their situation.

Circumstance-contingent theories enable managers to understand what it is about their present situation that has enabled their strategies and tactics to succeed. And they help managers recognize when important circumstances in their competitive environment are shifting so they can begin "piloting their plane" differently to sustain their success in the new circumstance. Theories that have advanced to this stage can help make success not only possible and predictable but sustainable. The work of building ever-better theory is never finished. As valuable as Porter's theory of clusters has proven, for example, there is a great opportunity for a researcher now to step in and find out when and why clusters that seem robust can disintegrate. That will lead to an even more robust theory of international competitive advantage.

The Importance of Failures

Note how critical it is for researchers, once they have hypothesized a causal mechanism, to identify circumstances in which companies did exactly what was prescribed but failed. Unfortunately, many management researchers are so focused on how companies succeed that they don't study failure. The obsession with studying successful companies and their "best practices" is a major reason why platitudes and fads in management come and go with such alarming regularity and why much early-stage management thinking doesn't evolve to the next stage. Managers try advice out because it sounds good and then discard it when they encounter circumstances in which the recommended actions do not yield the predicted results. Their conclusion most often is, "It doesn't work."

The question, "When *doesn't* it work?" is a magical key that enables statements of causality to be expressed in circumstance-contingent ways. For reasons we don't fully understand, many management researchers and writers are afraid to turn that key. As a consequence, many a promising stream of research has fallen into disuse and disrepute because its proponents carelessly claimed it would work in every instance instead of seeking to learn when it would work, when it wouldn't, and why.

In a good doctor-patient relationship, doctors usually can analyze and diagnose what is wrong with a specific patient and prescribe an appropriate therapy. By contrast, the relationship between managers, on the one hand, and those who research and write about management, on the other, is a distant one. If it is going to be useful, research must be conducted and written in ways that make it possible for readers to diagnose their situation themselves. When managers ask questions like, "Does this apply to my industry?" or "Does it apply to service businesses as well as product businesses?" they really are probing to understand the circumstances under which a theory does and does not work. Most of them have been burned by misapplied theory before. To know unambiguously what circumstance they *are* in, managers need also to know what circumstances they are *not* in. That is why getting the circumstance-defined categories right is so important in the process of building useful theory.

In our studies, we have observed that industry-based or product-versus-service-based categorization schemes almost never constitute a useful foundation for reliable theory because the circumstances that make a theory fail or succeed rarely coincide with industry boundaries. *The Innovator's Dilemma,* for example, described how precisely the same mechanism that enabled upstart companies to upend the leading, established firms in disk drives and computers also toppled the leading companies in mechanical excavators, steel, retailing, motorcycles, and accounting software. The circumstances that matter to this theory have nothing to do with what industry a company is in. They have to do with whether an innovation is or is not financially attractive to a company's business model. The mechanism—the resource allocation process—causes the established leaders to win the competitive fights when an innovation is financially attractive to their business model. And the same mechanism disables them when they are attacked by disruptive innovators whose products, profit models, and customers are not attractive to their model.

We can trust a theory only when, as in this example, its statement describing the actions that must lead to success explains how they will vary as a company's circumstances change. This is a major reason why the world of innovating managers has seemed quite random—because shoddy categorization by researchers has led to one-size-fits-all recommendations that have led to poor results in many circumstances. Not until we begin developing theories that managers can use in a circumstance-contingent way will we bring predictable success to the world of management.

Let's return to the Lucent example. The company is now in recovery: Market share in key product groups has stabilized, customers report increased satisfaction, and the stock price is recovering. Much of the turnaround seems to have been the result, in a tragic irony, not just of undoing the reorganization of the 1990s but of moving to a still more centralized structure. The current management team explicitly recognized the damage the earlier decentralization initiatives created and, guided by a theory that is appropriate to the complexity of Lucent's products and markets, has been working hard to put back in place an efficient structure that is aligned with the needs of Lucent's underlying technologies and products.

The moral of this story is that in business, as in medicine, no single prescription cures all ills. Lucent's managers felt pressured to grow in the 1990s. Lucent had a relatively centralized decision-making structure and its fair share of bureaucracy. Because most of the fast-growing technology companies of the day were comparatively unencumbered with such structures, management concluded that it should mimic them—a belief not only endorsed but promulgated by a number of management researchers. What got overlooked, with disastrous consequences, was that Lucent was emulating the attributes of small, fast-growing companies when its circumstances were fundamentally different. The management needed a theory to guide it to the organizational structure that was optimal for the circumstances the company was actually in.

Becoming a Discerning Consumer of Theory

Managers with a problem to solve will want to cut to the chase: Which theory will help them? How can they tell a good theory from a bad one? That is, when is a theory sufficiently well developed that its categorization scheme is indeed based not on coincidences but on causal links between circumstances, action, and results? Here are some ideas to help you judge how appropriate any theory or set of recommendations will be for your company's situation.

- When researchers are just beginning to study a problem or business issue, articles that simply describe the phenomenon can become an extremely valuable foundation for subsequent researchers' attempts to define categories and then to explain what causes the phenomenon to occur. For example, early work by Ananth Raman and his colleagues shook the world of supply chain studies simply by showing that companies with even the most sophisticated bar code–scanning systems had notoriously inaccurate inventory records. These observations led them to the next stage, in which they classified the types of errors the scanning systems produced and the sorts of stores in which those kinds of errors most often occurred. Raman and his colleagues then began carefully observing stocking processes to see exactly what kinds of behaviors could cause these errors. From this foundation, then, a theory explaining what systems work under what circumstances can emerge.

- Beware of work urging that revolutionary change of everything is needed. This is the fallacy of jumping directly from description to theory. If the authors imply that their findings apply to all companies in all situations, don't trust them. Usually things are the way they are for pretty good reasons. We need to know not only where, when, and why things must change but also what should stay the same. Most of the time, new categorization schemes don't completely overturn established thinking. Rather, they bring new insight into how to think and act in circumstance-contingent ways. Porter's work on international competitiveness, for example, did not overthrow preexisting trade theory but rather identified a circumstance in which a different mechanism of action led to competitive advantage.

- If the authors classify the phenomenon they're describing into categories based upon its attributes, simply accept that the study represents only a preliminary step toward a reliable theory. The most you can know at this stage is that there is some relationship between the characteristics of the companies being studied and the outcomes they experience. These can be described in terms of a general tendency of a population (20% of all companies funded by venture capital become successful; fewer of those funded by corporate capital do). But, if used to guide the actions of your individual company, they can easily send you on a wing-flapping expedition.

- Correlations that masquerade as causation often take the form of adjectives—*humble* CEOs create shareholder value, for instance, or *venture-capital* funding helps start-ups succeed. But a real theory should include a mechanism—a description of how something works. So a theory of how funding helps start-ups succeed might suggest that what venture capitalists do that makes the difference is meter out small amounts of funds to help the companies feel their way, step by step, toward a viable strategy. Funding in this way encourages start-ups to abandon unsuccessful initiatives right away and try new approaches. What corporate capitalists often do that's less effective is to flood a new business with a lot of money initially, allowing it to pursue the wrong strategy far longer. Then they pull the plug, thus preventing it from trying different approaches to find out what will work. During the dot-com boom, when venture capitalists flooded startups with money, the fact that it was venture money *per se* didn't help avert the predictable disaster.

- Remember that a researcher's findings can almost never be considered the final word. The discovery of a circumstance in which a theory did not accurately predict an outcome is a triumph, not a failure. Progress comes from refining theories to explain situations in which they previously failed, so without continuing our examination of failure, management theory cannot advance.

When Caveat Emptor Is Not Enough

In shopping for ideas, there is no Better Business Bureau managers can turn to for an assessment of how useful a given theory will be to them. Editors of management journals publish a range of different views on important issues—leaving it to the readers to decide which theories they should use to guide their actions.

But in the marketplace of ideas, caveat emptor—letting the reader beware—shirks the duty of research. For most managers, trying out a new idea to see if it works is simply not an option: There is too much at stake. Our hope is that an understanding of what constitutes good theory will help researchers do a better job of discovering the mechanisms that cause the outcomes managers care about, and that researchers will not be satisfied with measuring the statistical significance of correlations between attributes and outcomes. We hope they will see the value in asking, "When *doesn't* this work?" Researching that question will help them decipher the set of circumstances in which managers might find themselves and then frame contingent statements of cause and effect that take those circumstances into account.

We hope that a deeper understanding of what makes theory useful will enable editors to choose which pieces of research they will publish—and managers to choose which articles they will read and believe—on the basis of something other than authors' credentials or past successes. We hope that managers will exploit the fact that good theories can be judged on a more objective basis to make their "purchases" far more confidently.

Originally published in September 2003. Reprint R0309D

Note

1. Karl Popper asserted that when a researcher reaches the phase in which a theory accurately predicts what has been observed, the researcher can state only that the test or experiment "failed to disconfirm" the theory. See *The Logic of Scientific Discovery* (Harper & Row, 1968).

How Will You Measure Your Life?

by Clayton M. Christensen

BEFORE I PUBLISHED *The Innovator's Dilemma,* I got a call from Andrew Grove, then the chairman of Intel. He had read one of my early papers about disruptive technology, and he asked if I could talk to his direct reports and explain my research and what it implied for Intel. Excited, I flew to Silicon Valley and showed up at the appointed time, only to have Grove say, "Look, stuff has happened. We have only 10 minutes for you. Tell us what your model of disruption means for Intel." I said that I couldn't—that I needed a full 30 minutes to explain the model, because only with it as context would any comments about Intel make sense. Ten minutes into my explanation, Grove interrupted: "Look, I've got your model. Just tell us what it means for Intel."

I insisted that I needed 10 more minutes to describe how the process of disruption had worked its way through a very different industry, steel, so that he and his team could understand how disruption worked. I told the story of how Nucor and other steel minimills had begun by attacking the lowest end of the market—steel reinforcing bars, or rebar—and later moved up toward the high end, undercutting the traditional steel mills.

When I finished the minimill story, Grove said, "OK, I get it. What it means for Intel is ...," and then went on to articulate what would become the company's strategy for going to the bottom of the market to launch the Celeron processor.

I've thought about that a million times since. If I had been suckered into telling Andy Grove what he should think about the microprocessor business, I'd have been killed. But instead of telling him what to think, I taught him how to think—and then he reached what I felt was the correct decision on his own.

That experience had a profound influence on me. When people ask what I think they should do, I rarely answer their question directly. Instead, I run the question aloud through one of my models. I'll describe how the process in the model worked its way through an industry quite different from their own. And then, more often than not, they'll say, "OK, I get it." And they'll answer their own question more insightfully than I could have.

My class at HBS is structured to help my students understand what good management theory is and how it is built. To that backbone I attach different models or theories that help students think about the various dimensions of a general manager's job in stimulating innovation and growth. In each session we look at one company through the lenses of those theories—using them to explain how the company got into its situation and to examine what managerial actions will yield the needed results.

On the last day of class, I ask my students to turn those theoretical lenses on themselves, to find cogent answers to three questions: First, how can I be sure that I'll be happy in my career? Second, how can I be sure that my relationships with my spouse and my family become an enduring source of happiness? Third, how can I be sure I'll stay out of jail? Though the last question sounds lighthearted, it's not. Two of the 32 people in my Rhodes scholar class spent time in jail. Jeff Skilling of Enron fame was a classmate of mine at HBS. These were good guys—but something in their lives sent them off in the wrong direction.

As the students discuss the answers to these questions, I open my own life to them as a case study of sorts, to illustrate how they can use the theories from our course to guide their life decisions.

One of the theories that gives great insight on the first question—how to be sure we find happiness in our careers—is from Frederick Herzberg, who asserts that the powerful motivator in our lives isn't

Idea in Brief

Harvard Business School's Christensen teaches aspiring MBAs how to apply management and innovation theories to build stronger companies. But he also believes that these models can help people lead better lives. In this article, he explains how, exploring questions everyone needs to ask. How can I be happy in my career? How can I be sure that my relationship with my family is an enduring source of happiness? And how can I live my life with integrity? The answer to the first question comes from Frederick Herzberg's assertion that the most powerful motivator isn't money; it's the opportunity to learn, grow in responsibilities, contribute, and be recognized. That's why management, if practiced well, can be the noblest of occupations; no others offer as many ways to help people find those opportunities. It isn't about buying, selling, and investing in companies, as many think. The principles of resource allocation can help people attain happiness at home. If not managed masterfully, what emerges from a firm's resource allocation process can be very different from the strategy management intended to follow. That's true in life too: If you're not guided by a clear sense of purpose, you're likely to fritter away your time and energy on obtaining the most tangible, short-term signs of achievement, not what's really important to you. And just as a focus on marginal costs can cause bad corporate decisions, it can lead people astray. The marginal cost of doing something wrong "just this once" always seems alluringly low. You don't see the end result to which that path leads. The key is to define what you stand for and draw the line in a safe place.

money; it's the opportunity to learn, grow in responsibilities, contribute to others, and be recognized for achievements. I tell the students about a vision of sorts I had while I was running the company I founded before becoming an academic. In my mind's eye I saw one of my managers leave for work one morning with a relatively strong level of self-esteem. Then I pictured her driving home to her family 10 hours later, feeling unappreciated, frustrated, underutilized, and demeaned. I imagined how profoundly her lowered self-esteem affected the way she interacted with her children. The vision in my mind then fast-forwarded to another day, when she drove home with greater self-esteem—feeling that she had learned a lot, been recognized for achieving valuable things, and played a significant role in the success of some important initiatives. I then imagined how positively that affected her as a spouse and a parent. My conclusion: Management is the most noble of professions if it's practiced well. No other occupation offers as many ways to help others learn and grow, take responsibility and be recognized for achievement, and contribute to the success of a team. More and more MBA students come to school thinking that a career in business means buying, selling, and investing in companies. That's unfortunate. Doing deals doesn't yield the deep rewards that come from building up people.

I want students to leave my classroom knowing that.

Create a Strategy for Your Life

A theory that is helpful in answering the second question—How can I ensure that my relationship with my family proves to be an enduring source of happiness?—concerns how strategy is defined and implemented. Its primary insight is that a company's strategy is determined by the types of initiatives that management invests in. If a company's resource allocation process is not managed masterfully, what emerges from it can be very different from what management intended. Because companies' decision-making systems are designed to steer investments to initiatives that offer the most tangible and immediate returns, companies shortchange investments in initiatives that are crucial to their long-term strategies.

Over the years I've watched the fates of my HBS classmates from 1979 unfold; I've seen more and more of them come to reunions unhappy, divorced, and alienated from their children. I can guarantee you that not a single one of them graduated with the deliberate strategy of getting divorced and raising children who would become estranged from them. And yet a shocking number of them implemented that strategy. The reason? They didn't keep the purpose of their lives front and center as they decided how to spend their time, talents, and energy.

It's quite startling that a significant fraction of the 900 students that HBS draws each year from the world's best have given little thought to the purpose of their lives. I tell the students that HBS might be one of their last chances to reflect deeply on that question. If they think that they'll have more time and energy to reflect later, they're nuts, because life only gets more demanding: You take on a mortgage; you're working 70 hours a week; you have a spouse and children.

For me, having a clear purpose in my life has been essential. But it was something I had to think long and hard about before I understood it. When I was a Rhodes scholar, I was in a very demanding academic program, trying to cram an extra year's worth of work into my time at Oxford. I decided to spend an hour every night reading, thinking, and praying about why God put me on this earth. That was a very challenging commitment to keep, because every hour I spent doing that, I wasn't studying applied econometrics. I was conflicted about whether I could really afford to take that time away from my studies, but I stuck with it—and ultimately figured out the purpose of my life.

Had I instead spent that hour each day learning the latest techniques for mastering the problems of autocorrelation in regression analysis, I would have badly misspent my life. I apply the tools of econometrics a few times a year, but I apply my knowledge of the purpose of my life every day. It's the single most useful thing I've ever learned. I promise my students that if they take the time to figure out their life purpose, they'll look back on it as the most important thing they discovered at HBS. If they don't figure it out, they will just sail off without a rudder and get buffeted in the very rough seas of life. Clarity about their purpose will trump knowledge of activity-based costing, balanced scorecards, core competence, disruptive innovation, the four Ps, and the five forces.

My purpose grew out of my religious faith, but faith isn't the only thing that gives people direction. For example, one of my former students decided that his purpose was to bring honesty and economic prosperity to his country and to raise children who were as capably committed to this cause, and to each other, as he was. His purpose is focused on family and others—as mine is.

The choice and successful pursuit of a profession is but one tool for achieving your purpose. But without a purpose, life can become hollow.

The Class of 2010

"I CAME TO BUSINESS SCHOOL knowing exactly what I wanted to do—and I'm leaving choosing the exact opposite. I've worked in the private sector all my life, because everyone always told me that's where smart people are. But I've decided to try government and see if I can find more meaning there.

"I used to think that industry was very safe. The recession has shown us that nothing is safe."

Ruhana Hafiz, Harvard Business School, Class of 2010
Her Plans: To join the FBI as a special adviser (a management-track position)

"You could see a shift happening at HBS. Money used to be number one in the job search. When you make a ton of money, you want more of it. Ironic thing. You start to forget what the drivers of happiness are and what things are really important. A lot of people on campus see money differently now. They think, 'What's the minimum I need to have, and what else drives my life?' instead of 'What's the place where I can get the maximum of both?'"

Patrick Chun, Harvard Business School, Class of 2010
His Plans: To join Bain Capital

"The financial crisis helped me realize that you have to do what you really love in life. My current vision of success is based on the impact I can have, the experiences I can gain, and the happiness I can find personally, much more so than the pursuit of money or prestige. My main motivations are (1) to be with my family and people I care about; (2) to do something fun, exciting, and impactful; and (3) to pursue a long-term career in entrepreneurship, where I can build companies that change the way the world works."

Matt Salzberg, Harvard Business School, Class of 2010
His Plans: To work for Bessemer Venture Partners

"Because I'm returning to McKinsey, it probably seems like not all that much has changed for me. But while I was at HBS, I decided to do the dual degree at the Kennedy School. With the elections in 2008 and the economy looking shaky, it seemed more compelling for me to get a better understanding of the public and nonprofit sectors. In a way, that drove my return to McKinsey, where I'll have the ability to explore private, public, and nonprofit sectors.

"The recession has made us step back and take stock of how lucky we are. The crisis to us is 'Are we going to have a job by April?' Crisis to a lot of people is 'Are we going to stay in our home?'"

John Coleman, Harvard Business School, Class of 2010
His Plans: To return to McKinsey & Company

Allocate Your Resources

Your decisions about allocating your personal time, energy, and talent ultimately shape your life's strategy.

I have a bunch of "businesses" that compete for these resources: I'm trying to have a rewarding relationship with my wife, raise great kids, contribute to my community, succeed in my career, contribute to my church, and so on. And I have exactly the same problem that a corporation does. I have a limited amount of time and energy and talent. How much do I devote to each of these pursuits?

Allocation choices can make your life turn out to be very different from what you intended. Sometimes that's good: Opportunities that you never planned for emerge. But if you misinvest your resources, the outcome can be bad. As I think about my former classmates who inadvertently invested for lives of hollow unhappiness, I can't help believing that their troubles relate right back to a short-term perspective.

When people who have a high need for achievement—and that includes all Harvard Business School graduates—have an extra half hour of time or an extra ounce of energy, they'll unconsciously allocate it to activities that yield the most tangible accomplishments. And our careers provide the most concrete evidence that we're moving forward. You ship a product, finish a design, complete a presentation, close a sale, teach a class, publish a paper, get paid, get promoted. In contrast, investing time and energy in your relationship with your spouse and children typically doesn't offer that same immediate sense of achievement. Kids misbehave every day. It's really not until 20 years down the road that you can put your hands on your hips and say, "I raised a good son or a good daughter." You can neglect your relationship with your spouse, and on a day-to-day basis, it doesn't seem as if things are deteriorating. People who are driven to excel have this unconscious propensity to underinvest in their families and overinvest in their careers—even though intimate and loving relationships with their families are the most powerful and enduring source of happiness.

If you study the root causes of business disasters, over and over you'll find this predisposition toward endeavors that offer immediate gratification. If you look at personal lives through that lens, you'll see the same stunning and sobering pattern: people allocating fewer and fewer resources to the things they would have once said mattered most.

Create a Culture

There's an important model in our class called the Tools of Cooperation, which basically says that being a visionary manager isn't all it's cracked up to be. It's one thing to see into the foggy future with acuity and chart the course corrections that the company must make. But it's quite another to persuade employees who might not see the changes ahead to line up and work cooperatively to take the company in that new direction. Knowing what tools to wield to elicit the needed cooperation is a critical managerial skill.

The theory arrays these tools along two dimensions—the extent to which members of the organization agree on what they want from their participation in the enterprise, and the extent to which they agree on what actions will produce the desired results. When there is little agreement on both axes, you have to use "power tools"—coercion, threats, punishment, and so on—to secure cooperation. Many companies start in this quadrant, which is why the founding executive team must play such an assertive role in defining what must be done and how. If employees' ways of working together to address those tasks succeed over and over, consensus begins to form. MIT's Edgar Schein has described this process as the mechanism by which a culture is built. Ultimately, people don't even think about whether their way of doing things yields success. They embrace priorities and follow procedures by instinct and assumption rather than by explicit decision—which means that they've created a culture. Culture, in compelling but unspoken ways, dictates the proven, acceptable methods by which members of the group address recurrent problems. And culture defines the priority given to different types of problems. It can be a powerful management tool.

In using this model to address the question, How can I be sure that my family becomes an enduring source of happiness?, my students quickly see that the simplest tools that parents can wield to elicit cooperation from children are power tools. But there comes a point during the teen years when power tools no longer work. At that point parents start wishing that they had begun working with their children at a very young age to build a culture at home in which children instinctively behave respectfully toward one another, obey their parents, and choose the right thing to do. Families have cultures, just as companies do. Those cultures can be built consciously or evolve inadvertently.

If you want your kids to have strong self-esteem and confidence that they can solve hard problems, those qualities won't magically materialize in high school. You have to design them into your family's culture—and you have to think about this very early on. Like employees, children build self-esteem by doing things that are hard and learning what works.

Avoid the "Marginal Costs" Mistake

We're taught in finance and economics that in evaluating alternative investments, we should ignore sunk and fixed costs, and instead base decisions on the marginal costs and marginal revenues that each alternative entails. We learn in our course that this doctrine biases companies to leverage what they have put in place to succeed in the past, instead of guiding them to create the capabilities they'll need in the future. If we knew the future would be exactly the same as the past, that approach would be fine. But if the future's different—and it almost always is—then it's the wrong thing to do.

This theory addresses the third question I discuss with my students—how to live a life of integrity (stay out of jail). Unconsciously, we often employ the marginal cost doctrine in our personal lives when we choose between right and wrong. A voice in our head says, "Look, I know that as a general rule, most people shouldn't do this. But in this particular extenuating circumstance, just this once, it's OK." The marginal cost of doing something wrong "just this once" always seems alluringly low. It suckers you in, and you don't ever look at where that path ultimately is headed and at the full costs that the choice entails. Justification for infidelity and dishonesty in all their manifestations lies in the marginal cost economics of "just this once."

I'd like to share a story about how I came to understand the potential damage of "just this once" in my own life. I played on the Oxford University varsity basketball team. We worked our tails off and finished the season undefeated. The guys on the team were the best friends I've ever had in my life. We got to the British equivalent of the NCAA tournament—and made it to the final four. It turned out the championship game was scheduled to be played on a Sunday. I had made a personal commitment to God at age 16 that I would never play ball on Sunday. So I went to the coach and explained my problem. He was incredulous. My teammates were, too, because I was the starting center. Every one of the guys on the team came to me and said, "You've got to play. Can't you break the rule just this one time?"

I'm a deeply religious man, so I went away and prayed about what I should do. I got a very clear feeling that I shouldn't break my commitment—so I didn't play in the championship game.

In many ways that was a small decision—involving one of several thousand Sundays in my life. In theory, surely I could have crossed over the line just that one time and then not done it again. But looking back on it, resisting the temptation whose logic was "In this extenuating circumstance, just this once, it's OK" has proven to be one of the most important decisions of my life. Why? My life has been one unending stream of extenuating circumstances. Had I crossed the line that one time, I would have done it over and over in the years that followed.

The lesson I learned from this is that it's easier to hold to your principles 100% of the time than it is to hold to them 98% of the time. If you give in to "just this once," based on a marginal cost analysis, as some of my former classmates have done, you'll regret where you end up. You've got to define for yourself what you stand for and draw the line in a safe place.

Remember the Importance of Humility

I got this insight when I was asked to teach a class on humility at Harvard College. I asked all the students to describe the most humble person they knew. One characteristic of these humble people stood out: They had a high level of self-esteem. They knew who they were, and they felt good about who they were. We also decided that humility was defined not by self-deprecating behavior or attitudes but by the esteem with which you regard others. Good behavior flows naturally from that kind of humility. For example, you would never steal from someone, because you respect that person too much. You'd never lie to someone, either.

It's crucial to take a sense of humility into the world. By the time you make it to a top graduate school, almost all your learning has come from people who are smarter and more experienced than you: parents, teachers, bosses. But once you've finished at Harvard Business School or any other top academic institution, the vast majority of people you'll interact with on a day-to-day basis may not be smarter than you. And if your attitude is that only smarter people have something to teach you, your learning opportunities will be very limited. But if you have a humble eagerness to learn something from everybody, your learning opportunities will be unlimited. Generally, you can be humble only if you feel really good about yourself—and you want to help those around you feel really good about themselves, too. When we see people acting in an abusive, arrogant, or demeaning manner toward others, their behavior almost always is a symptom of their lack of self-esteem. They need to put someone else down to feel good about themselves.

Choose the Right Yardstick

This past year I was diagnosed with cancer and faced the possibility that my life would end sooner than I'd planned. Thankfully, it now looks as if I'll be spared. But the experience has given me important insight into my life.

I have a pretty clear idea of how my ideas have generated enormous revenue for companies that have used my research; I know I've had a substantial impact. But as I've confronted this disease, it's been interesting to see how unimportant that impact is to me now. I've concluded that the metric by which God will assess my life isn't dollars but the individual people whose lives I've touched.

I think that's the way it will work for us all. Don't worry about the level of individual prominence you have achieved; worry about the individuals you have helped become better people. This is my final recommendation: Think about the metric by which your life will be judged, and make a resolution to live every day so that in the end, your life will be judged a success.

Originally published in July 2010. Reprint R1007B

About the Contributors

CLAYTON M. CHRISTENSEN is the Kim B. Clark Professor of Business Administration at Harvard Business School. In addition to his most recent volume, *How Will You Measure Your Life?*, he has authored seven critically acclaimed books, including several *New York Times* bestsellers: *The Innovator's Dilemma, The Innovator's Solution,* and, most recently, *Disrupting Class.* Christensen is the cofounder of Innosight, a global strategy and innovation consultancy; Rose Park Advisors, an investment firm; and the Clayton Christensen Institute for Disruptive Innovation, a nonprofit think tank. In 2011 and 2013, Christensen was named the world's most influential business thinker by Thinkers50.

RICHARD ALTON is a senior researcher at the Forum for Growth and Innovation at Harvard Business School.

JOSEPH L. BOWER is the Donald Kirk David Professor of Business Administration at Harvard Business School.

SCOTT COOK is the cofounder and chairman of Intuit, based in Mountain View, California.

TADDY HALL is the chief strategy officer of the Advertising Research Foundation in New York City.

MARK W. JOHNSON is the chairman and a cofounder of Innosight, a strategic innovation and investing company based in Boston.

HENNING KAGERMANN is a former CEO of SAP AG, a software corporation based in Germany.

STEPHEN P. KAUFMAN, a senior lecturer at Harvard Business School, is the retired chairman and CEO of Arrow Electronics.

RORY MCDONALD is an assistant professor at Harvard Business School.

MICHAEL OVERDORF is a Dean's Research Fellow at Harvard Business School.

MICHAEL E. RAYNOR is a director with Deloitte Research, and a professor at the Richard Ivey School of Business in London, Ontario, Canada.

CURTIS RISING is the managing director of Harvard Square Partners, a consulting practice focused on inorganic growth and leadership assessment and based in Cambridge, Massachusetts.

WILLY C. SHIH is a professor of management practice at Harvard Business School. He held executive positions at IBM, Silicon Graphics, and Kodak.

MATTHEW VERLINDEN is a manager at Integral, an international strategy consulting firm based in Cambridge, Massachusetts.

ANDREW WALDECK is a partner at Innosight, an innovation and strategy consulting firm in Watertown, Massachusetts.

MAXWELL WESSEL is a fellow at the Forum for Growth and Innovation and a senior researcher at Harvard Business School.

Index